CASSANDRA PYBUS

GROSS MORAL TURPITUDE

THE ORR CASE RECONSIDERED

untapped

ABOUT *UNTAPPED*

Most Australian books ever written have fallen out of print and become unavailable for purchase or loan from libraries. This includes important local and national histories, biographies and memoirs, beloved children's titles, and even winners of glittering literary prizes such as the Miles Franklin Literary Award.

Supported by funding from state and territory libraries, philanthropists and the Australian Research Council, *Untapped* is identifying Australia's culturally important lost books, digitising them, and promoting them to new generations of readers. As well as providing access to lost books and a new source of revenue for their writers, the *Untapped* collaboration is supporting new research into the economic value of authors' reversion rights and book promotion by libraries, and the relationship between library lending and digital book sales. The results will feed into public policy discussions about how we can better support Australian authors, readers and culture.

See untapped.org.au for more information, including a full list of project partners and rediscovered books.

Readers are reminded that these books are products of their time. Some may contain language or reflect views that might now be found offensive or inappropriate.

for Lucy Frost

CONTENTS

ACKNOWLEDGEMENTS

Researching this book has made me realise what sterling people are archivists. My thanks go to Ken Smith, archivist, Sydney University; Shirley King, archivist, University of Tasmania; Michael Saclier, archivist, Business and Labour Archives, Australian National University, and Robert Smart, Keeper of the Muniments at St Andrews University, Scotland. For Frank Strahan, the splendid archivist of Melbourne University I reserve a special, heartfelt thanks. My regrets, too, that despite his best efforts I was not permitted access to the papers of SS Orr, in the Melbourne University archives.

I must also record my appreciation for the assistance of Professor Alan Gilbert, Vice-Chancellor of the University of Tasmania and the University Secretary, Ross Skinner. As well my thanks go to Gwen Harwood, Meriel Wright, John Biggs, Shirley and Jan Tanner, Henry Findlay and to the many people who were so willing to share their memories. I am grateful for the grants from the Literature Board of the Australia Council and the Minister for Education and Arts through Arts Tasmania, which greatly assisted the research and writing of this book in 1992.

LIST OF CHARACTERS

Geoffrey Allison Chemistry student at the University of Tasmania in 1955. Appointed demonstrator in chemistry in 1956. Gave evidence against Orr. Married Suzanne Kemp in 1958. Set up a chemical testing business in Hobart.

Paul Berry ABC radio announcer during Orr case. Member of Scots Kirk 1956–58. One of the citizens committee formed to support Orr.

John Biggs Student of Orr's in 1945 and 1955. Gave evidence in support of Orr to Supreme Court and to the Scots Kirk.

Ken Buckley Secretary of Federal Council of University Staff Associations (FCUSA) 1957–58, 1960–61.

Stanley Burbury Solicitor-general in Tasmania 1955–56. Succeeded Sir John Morris as chief justice. Member of the university council. Knighted in 1958.

Sam Warren Carey Professor of geology at University of Tasmania from 1946. Internationally acclaimed geologist. Chairman of the professorial board 1954–56. Active in staff association. Took a leading role in royal commission into the university administration. Established a fund for Orr family after Orr's death.

Alf Conlon Leader of a legendary research unit during the war which included Panzee Wright, Isles, McAuley and Kerr. Had a reputation as the doyen of backroom operators in Sydney in the 1950s and 1960s.

Bishop Cranswick Counsellor to Orr 1952–53. Expressed concern about Orr's morality to the university in 1955. Later claimed to have been deliberately misled by the university's legal advisor and called for new inquiry.

Ken Dallas Lecturer in economics at the University of Tasmania. While not a member of the communist party, had strong left-wing political associations.

Hector Dunn Moderator of the Scots Kirk Session 1956–61. Enthusiastic Orr supporter. Initiated an inquiry into Orr case through the Kirk.

WHC (Harry) Eddy Senior tutor in extension courses at Sydney University. Author of a major analysis of the Orr case in 1961. Very close to Orr, who lived with him 1960–61.

Frederick Eggleston Distinguished lawyer, diplomat, writer and liberal intellectual who had been very influential in the establishment of the Australian National University. Knighted in 1941. Died 1954.

Gerald Firth Professor of economics at the University of Tasmania from 1947. Active in staff association and royal commission.

Alexander Boyce Gibson Professor of philosophy at Melbourne University from 1935. Appointed Orr to lectureship at Melbourne in 1947. Referee for Orr in 1951. Opposed Australian Association of Philosophers' support for Orr.

William (Bill) Ginnane Lecturer in philosophy at Sydney University, then at the Australian National University. Strong supporter of Orr within the AAP.

Kenneth Green Supreme Court judge. Heard the case *Orr vs University of Tasmania* in 1956. Knighted in 1957.

Geoffrey Harrison University of Tasmania accountant in 1950s. Active in staff association and royal commission.

Gwen Harwood Australian poet. Married to Bill Harwood, lecturer in English during the Orr case. Close friend of Edwin Tanner.

Malcolm Hills President of Student Representative Council at the University of Tasmania in 1956. Gave evidence for Orr at the Supreme Court and the Scots Kirk. Remained a strong Orr supporter.

William Hodgman MHA for Denison from 1955. Orr's solicitor and junior barrister in Supreme Court case.

Donald Horne Freelance writer and editor. Published the *Observer.* Became editor of the *Bulletin.*

Torleiv Hytten Born in Norway. Economics advisor to the Bank of NSW 1935–49. Vice-chancellor of the University of Tasmania 1949–57.

Keith Isles Tasmanian graduate who became professor of economics at Queen's University, Belfast. Returned to Tasmania as vice-chancellor in 1957. Sued by Orr in every Australian state, the United Kingdom and New Zealand.

Tony Kearney Assistant registrar at University of Tasmania in 1950s. Active in staff association and royal commission.

Suzanne Kemp Student at the University of Tasmania in 1954–55, majoring in philosophy, French and German. Complained in March 1956 that Orr had seduced her. Daughter of a prominent timber merchant, Reginald Kemp. Married Geoffrey Allison in 1958.

John Kerr Distinguished lawyer and prominent member of the Australian Council for Cultural Freedom until his resignation in 1961. He reviewed the Supreme Court evidence with Hal Wootten. Became Governor General in 1974.

Phillip Lake Philosophy student. Lived briefly in a ground-floor flat in Orr's house after 1956. Gave evidence in support of Orr at the Supreme Court.

John Latham Chief Justice of the High Court 1935–52, after a successful political career, and president of the Australian Council for Cultural Freedom till 1961. Friend of John Morris.

Jan Locher Czech-born student majoring in philosophy, psychology and history. Close to Orr in 1956. Gave evidence in support of Orr at the Supreme Court.

Alexander Macbeath Professor of philosophy at Queen's University, Belfast, until 1960. Supervisor for Orr. Spent eighteen months as visiting professor of philosophy at Tasmania 1960–61.

Malcolm McCrae Lecturer in history at University of Tasmania. Active in staff association and was secretary during royal commission and Orr case. Vocal critic of the university administration. Strong supporter of Orr.

James McAuley Australian poet. First editor of *Quadrant*. Reader in poetry at Tasmania in 1959, later professor of English. Chairman of the professorial board during negotiations for a final settlement of the Orr case.

Kajica Milanov Born in Yugoslavia. Briefly professor of philosophy at Belgrade, 1945–46. Migrated to Tasmania from displaced person's camp in Austria 1953. Appointed lecturer in philosophy in Tasmania in 1954. Complained of harassment by Orr.

John Montrose Lecturer in law at Queen's University, Belfast. Interested in implications of the master-servant finding in Orr case.

Edmund Morris Miller Professor of psychology and philosophy at University of Tasmania 1922–52. Part-time vice-chancellor 1933–45. Regarded as a leading intellectual progressive between the wars.

John Morris Chief Justice of the Supreme Court of Tasmania 1940–56. Knighted in 1943. Elected chancellor of the university in 1944. Chairman of the Adult Education Board. Criticised by the royal commission in 1954. Died, aged 54, in 1956.

Sydney Sparkes Orr Born in Ireland. Graduate of Queen's University, Belfast. Lecturer in philosophy at St Andrews, Scotland, and Melbourne. Appointed professor of philosophy at Tasmania in 1952. Active in staff association and royal commission. Dismissed for misconduct in 1956. Died in August 1966.

John Bela Polya Born in Hungary. Associate professor of chemistry at the University of Tasmania. Active in the staff association and vocal critic of the administration. Close associate of Orr at the university.

Alan Ker Stout Professor of moral and political philosophy at Sydney University from 1939. President of the Australian Association of Philosophers throughout the Orr case. Spearheaded ban on the chair of philosophy in Tasmania after Orr's dismissal.

Edwin Tanner Senior engineer at Hydro-Electricity Commission till 1957. Part-time philosophy student at the University of Tasmania 1954–56. MA student at Monash University in 1960s. Complained that Orr had sought favours in return for academic preferment. An established artist represented in major collections throughout Australia.

Wilfred Asquith Townsley Lecturer in history at the University of Tasmania from 1945. Appointed foundation professor of political science, without advertisement, following his unsuccessful application for chair of history in 1956. Complained of harassment by Orr.

Edward (Ted) Wheelwright The first secretary of Federal Council of University Staff Associations. Became first editor of *Vestes.*

Hal Wootten Distinguished lawyer who, together with John Kerr (later Governor-General), reviewed Supreme Court evidence during 1957.

JN Wright Professor of philosophy at St Andrews, Scotland, who refused to renew Orr's lectureship in 1942.

Reginald Wright Liberal Senator for Tasmania from 1950. University of Tasmania's barrister and legal advisor.

Roy Douglas (Panzee) Wright Brother of Reginald. Professor of physiology at Melbourne University from 1939. Acted as Orr's 'next friend'. Became chancellor of Melbourne University in 1980.

Guildford Young Catholic archbishop in Tasmania from 1955. Supported Orr until 1962. Called for a new inquiry.

'Men who allow their love of power to give them a distorted view of the world are to be found in every asylum; one man will think he is the Governor of the Bank of England, another will think he is the King, and yet another will think he is God. Highly similar delusions, if expressed by educated men in obscure language, lead to professorships in philosophy ...'

Bertrand Russell

'My integrity has been called into question by people who have never spoken to me.'

Anita Hill during US Senate hearings on judge-elect Clarence Thomas

CHAPTER ONE

Either love is supreme and good, or it's not

It was Boxing Day at Orford, Tasmania, in 1955. Squalling winds blew in from the Tasman Sea across the steel-grey waters of Prosser Bay. The beach was out of the question, while the fishing fraternity which dominated the sheltered anchorages of the river mouth held no interest for a languid nineteen-year-old with romantic longings. Besides, Suzanne Kemp had a terrible toothache. Her head and jaw throbbed with the onset of a wisdom tooth. Her university exams were over and the holidays barely begun, but already she was overcome with ennui, flattened by vague discontent and fears which she could not fathom. The dismal weather suited her mood.

She roused from her listlessness to consider Geoffrey Allison, due to arrive next day for a visit. She'd been seeing him on and off for the last few months and found him sensitive and insightful, even though he was a science student; but with so much on her mind, quite apart from toothache, she felt his visit was inauspicious.

Geoffrey Allison came to Orford with mixed feelings. Certainly he liked Suzanne. She was very intelligent and, unlike a lot of girls her age, she liked to talk about serious things like politics; things that really mattered. And she was pretty, with round, rosy cheeks and lovely dark eyes. But it was not Suzanne Kemp's conversation and good looks that drew Geoffrey to Orford. He was seriously concerned about her state of mind. At a student party three months earlier he'd first noticed that she seemed troubled, but he hadn't been able to get to the bottom of it, despite his subtle probing on their occasional dates. In

December, during a trip to the Huon River, Suzanne was so distracted he'd asked straight out what was on her mind. Why, he had wanted to know, was she acting so strangely and why had she been so evasive when he had suggested other outings and activities?

Suzanne was really quite relieved to have him ask. She was in a bit of bother, she confessed, because she had told her parents that Geoffrey had taken her out to the beach two days before, whereas, in fact, she had been there with a certain person, a married man who lived in Hobart with his family. Since her parents would likely ask Geoffrey about it, she was worried that her deception might be exposed. He was left to deduce that the unidentified married man lay at the heart of the distractions and evasions he found so worrying. It was far from reassuring, this startling confession of an affair with a married man. In his mind there was no doubt that Suzanne was a girl in trouble and she needed his help. He was not trying to play at psychology; it was a matter of common sense. Suzanne was very young and vulnerable. She was clearly being disturbed by her clandestine relationship and no possible good could come of it. By the time he left Hobart for the holiday at Orford, Geoffrey Allison was pretty sure he had guessed the identity of Suzanne's unnamed married lover. That deduction made him even more alarmed for her well-being.

Throughout the six days he stayed at Orford with the Kemp family, Geoffrey felt ill-at-ease. Suzanne did nothing to make his stay especially pleasant, remaining withdrawn and uncommunicative until he left. Attempts to get her to open up about her preoccupations got him nowhere. Cooped up in the house by the bad weather they began to get on each other's nerves. One time he did manage to kiss her, but this got him no closer to the revelations he had hoped for. On Tuesday 2 January, when Suzanne had taken to her sickbed, he left for home, none the wiser.

The following Thursday evening, alone in the house and

recovered from her toothache, Suzanne was a good deal more forthcoming about her feelings and her motivations. 'My dear Sydney,' she wrote:

> Just as well I haven't written to you before. You would have been horrified at the results of my rationalising. It is surprising what a few days of almost solitary confinement in dismal weather coupled with head and tooth ache can do to one's reason. I have been in bed since Tuesday, the cause being as far as I can see the coming of a wisdom tooth. Being the last one, it decided it wouldn't fight the last fight without some show for it. What agonies I must have suffered when I was a baby. I am better now except for being rather weak in the head and shaky in the hand. I am sure this is the simple explanation of my illness, but Geoff said in an intense and significant voice that he thought it was 'something far deeper than that'. Probably the fact that I went to bed late the night before and had no sleep the night before that (New Year's Eve). Anyway don't worry. In my present state of convalescence I am devouring books, and I doubt I will be completely better until I am out or the weather improves. Good weather for painting—I hope your job seems to be growing smaller instead of larger, but I rather fear the latter.
>
> I suppose you want to hear about Geoff's stay. Of course the weather was impossible so we couldn't do much. He is a very active person who has to be doing something or going somewhere so the inactivity may have made him a bit jittery. We got into the most impossible situations and tangles with words, saying things with hidden meanings and goodness knows what, interspersed by him (with a peculiar intonation) 'I don't know what the future holds' ... (Obviously he

has had his whole life planned and I have come along and wrecked it) or by me with a sudden blunt statement in exasperation. He sees me as a very absent, indifferent creature with vacant eyes, who is never in the present situation, but who lives at some subterranean depth with deep and hidden care and sorrow and deep and hidden violent emotions. He feels he can't cope with the situation because I am never there 'If only I could do something—if *only* I could find the real You'—He tried in a timid way by making love to me, but said, after a bit of questioning by me, that he found it 'rather humiliating' to make love to someone who doesn't love him. He is right there. He is really very sensitive and intelligent and clear-sighted (we had a very long discussion about the corruption and abuse of power in Tasmania, about which he knows a lot more than I do) and I like him to do things with, but apart from that, I don't know. He is right when he says I am not 'there'. I am usually chasing a piece of music
'down the nights and down the days
down the labyrinthine ways
of my own mind'
and I can't help it. I just unconsciously start singing inside myself and I am gone in a minute. Some little devil wafts me off to music land and I am quite indifferent to (though not absolutely unconscious of) the suffering of the person next to me. I hope I don't sound too frivolous. The position is serious, at least for him. He knows exactly what will happen before he comes near me, and yet he keeps coming back for more. I can't understand it. Either love is supreme and good, or it's not, and how could one believe it was if one's first experience brought only bitterness, hopelessness, frustration? (My fault?) I have allowed a situ-

ation to develop which I am not prepared to handle? I don't know. He knew the situation before we even started but he wants to do something constructive. Build. Plan the future, but I am afraid the foundations aren't very sound. I don't help just sitting singing really, do I? (I can feel your rather disapproving expression from here.) You said once that you believed one didn't really love unless it was returned. Well, either he doesn't really love me, or I love him but won't admit it. The former you hope? It doesn't seem like it to me. He has been in an odd state for months. There seems to be too many exceptions to that statement. But then if it is not true so much love can be fruitless and the ideal weakens considerably. Ah well, having reached this point I feel I have wandered enough. Fiddling with abstracts—almost as good an escape as singing ('escaping' is becoming a mania with me). Anyway, no doubt Geoff is back at work with a rather glazed expression trying to find a way through my impassive surface to the subterranean emotions beneath. And I? As you see I am doing nothing AS USUAL.

And what about you? Neglected and forgotten? I think a shrug of the shoulders would be appropriate here. As I said, my tooth played havoc with my reason, and you haunted me in fiendish forms. Ah my dear, I am young and foolish. Forgive me for I know not what I do. Don't expect too much of me. I can feel how much you depend on and are sustained by love and it rather frightens me. It gives me so much power. But you have not that power over me, or not so much. It is true that you have changed me, that your outlook on life and mine have in me become so mixed that I cannot separate them, and I love you as much as I know how at this moment. But you haven't touched my very being, even though you are the centre of my life. Maybe no one ever will. Maybe I would never give it.

Do you believe me? Do you think it is my childish streak coming through to hurt? It is what I feel, have always felt, whatever it is.

I am rather hungry. My parents have gone to a communal gathering and it's 9 o'clock and I haven't had any tea. These gatherings take place every night in various houses and get later and later. Very wisely we had one here first which ended at 7.30. They, at least my father, seem to drink a little more each time too. I don't blame them, there is nothing else to do in such weather. I usually go, but haven't been able to lately. Geoff went to a few and wondered how I, being so unusual and distant, could bear (bare?) to make small talk to rather uninteresting people over a glass of beer. Seen through an outsider's eyes it is rather ridiculous but for once, thank goodness I am not an outsider. All the odd attachments I have for some of these people! Otherwise, of course, there would be no sense in coming here year after year.

I don't know when I will be coming to town again. I foresee nothing as yet. I feel no desperate need to be with you, except when I think of Christ. No doubt this has very interesting psychological implications (I hope not too awful) which I am afraid I can't work out. Perhaps you and He have unconsciously swapped places in my mind. No doubt if you took a sample of my handwriting to a specialist he could give you some interesting psychological data too.

I had better stop as I become rather dramatic and peculiar as the night wears on. I know how violently you react to what I think are quite harmless statements, so I will keep my midnight musings to myself.

I hope the New Year hasn't brought anything drastic for you.

Please give my love to your family.
Yours,
Suzanne.

That letter reached Professor Sydney Sparkes Orr of the philosophy department at the University of Tasmania on 5 January 1956. He dated the letter in his own hand, making the common mistake of using the date of the year just finished. He may have read the letter several times before penning a short reply, since he later said 'It was the most puzzling and disturbing letter I had received in my life.' After further reflection he wrote another letter, which Suzanne received a few days later than the first. Both letters were destroyed. Professor Orr did not destroy Suzanne's disturbing missive, however. Nor did he seek advice from anyone about the contents he found so puzzling. Bishop Cranswick, from whom he had sought counsel through the previous years, was not consulted, nor was the vice-chancellor, nor the university chaplain nor any person responsible for student welfare at the university. Neither did he approach Suzanne's parents. Instead he kept the letter in the pocket of his jacket, where he found it again some six months later, after a request from the university's lawyers.

Had Geoffrey Allison stayed at the Kemp holiday house long enough to observe Suzanne posting letters to and receiving letters from the professor of philosophy he might have felt some small satisfaction, for this was indeed the lover he had surmised, and his mounting concern for Suzanne was fuelled by rumours he had heard about Orr's private life. These same rumours reached Reginald Kemp, Suzanne's father, when he returned to his Hobart timber business in mid-January. His friend KJ Binns told him that Orr was an undesirable character who had got girls into trouble in Melbourne. The story about Orr's behaviour in Melbourne had been brought to light at a university council meeting Binns had attended in December and was the cause of the writs for defamation that Orr had issued against four fellow professors, three of whom were also members of the university council. Knowing that Suzanne was a student of Orr's, Binns warned his friend he should see to it that she had nothing more to do with him.

Reginald Kemp was not especially alarmed by his conversation with Mr Binns. He knew his daughter to be very supportive of Orr and active in university doings, especially as secretary of the student Socratic Club, but he saw no reason to fear her association with Orr, who had dropped around to the Kemp house one Sunday morning to apologise for keeping Suzanne late at a Socratic Club meeting. When the professor reappeared the following Sunday morning they had shared an amiable beer and chat. Still, it was an unsavoury matter, so when the family returned, Kemp told his wife of Binns' story and asked her to speak to Suzanne.

Suzanne was thrown into turmoil by her mother's revelations. Not that the allegations were entirely new to her. Almost a year ago a friend had repeated some story she had heard from her father, who was a judge, that Professor Orr had had to leave Melbourne because he had seduced a girl and she was not the first. At that time Suzanne had found the story mildly titillating; it had increased her interest in the charismatic professor. Writing in her occasional diary she confided, 'I can believe it and feel a peculiar excitement. I don't admire him much ... Is he honourable? If I can expect anything from him, then I am afraid he will completely lose my respect and do I want him to?' That was before she really got close to Orr. Now she saw this gossip as an unprincipled attempt to undermine his credibility as a critic of the university authorities. That her own father, who had nothing to do with the university, should be party to this process made her very hurt and angry. She took her anger and distress around to the Orr house in Hamilton Street, where she was a familiar visitor. Over supper she and Sydney, together with his wife Sadie, discussed the story from Mr Binns and her father's reaction.

By this time the story was common knowledge to Sydney Orr. He had issued a series of writs to try to stop it. These writs were the only way he had to defend himself, he explained to Suzanne, because people were making allegations about him and investigating him in secret. He made no suggestion of issuing writs against her father, or his friend, but he did emphasise that he needed students like her, who believed in him, to support him, as she had already done by writing a testimonial before she left for Orford. She could help him even further if she were to write another letter touching upon the matters Mr Binns had raised with her father. Suzanne could already see the dangers in this, and she was getting increasingly uneasy about her relationship with Sydney, but she was unswerving in her belief in him and would do everything she could to help.

After she had driven home in her mother's car, Suzanne allowed herself a quiver of doubt about Orr. Somehow he no longer seemed so impressive, or so fearless. Around the edges of her consciousness she experienced a quickening sensation of divergence. This was not the first time. As early as August she had written in her diary:

> Do you know I feel sort of disgusted when I have to meet you at night—just the fact that I am waiting in the dark and you come and I have to walk to your car—you have the ideas, the feelings but not quite the strength of personality to give them meaning and existence ... your fight becomes a banal discarding and contempt of convention more bounded by convention than the man who never gives it a thought.

Of course she did love him, but she could not entirely suppress the doubt: *What if what they say about him is true*?

A few days later, on Sunday 19 February, she took a phone call from Malcolm Hills, president of the Students' Representative Council. Would she go to the Orr house in Hamilton Street that afternoon to make a statement to Orr's legal advisor? he requested. Suzanne was elated at the opportunity to dispel the disloyal sensations which had begun to assail her. Still, she was taken aback, and momentarily hurt, that Hills, who was just another student, had been told what she had said about Mr Binns in her very intimate discussions with Sydney. She appeared so flustered as she passed through the living room after taking the call that her father wanted to know what it had been about. He was told Suzanne intended to go to Professor Orr's place to make a statement on his behalf. Reginald Kemp was implacably opposed to the idea. He was not having his daughter mixed up in Orr's unpleasantness, and he phoned the professor to tell him so, explaining that if it were simply a matter of Suzanne making a statement that her relationship with the professor was quite in order, as other girls were doing, she could do this providing he was also present. Reginald Kemp had no intention of finding himself on the receiving end of one of Orr's defamation writs.

Suzanne was incensed. She shut herself in her room and dashed off a furious note to Malcolm Hills. Her father was behaving fanatically, she explained: 'I think he is being doped up by the other side.' At the same time she drafted another statement explaining why she had been unable to defend herself against statements about herself and Professor Orr and detailing the allegation made against Orr by her father's friend.

On Monday night she took the draft to Hamilton Street so that Orr could check what she had written. Confident she had now done the right thing by him, she sealed her statement, enclosing it with a covering note. A fellow student collected it from Suzanne on Tuesday the 21st to give to Malcolm Hills. On Wednesday night Suzanne was back at Hamilton Street to discuss tactics. It was then that Mrs Orr, unhappy at the duplicity, urged Suzanne to tell her father what she had done.

Around nine o'clock that evening Reginald Kemp got a most unpleasant surprise when Suzanne marched into the living room and handed him a letter. Astounded, he read:

> You once said, 'I let you go your way. You let me go mine', and it's true. There is nothing else we can do. You don't understand nor want to understand my world, I can't become a part of yours. You believe in Mr Binns and what he says. You think it right that he should tell you things in confidence without proof, and you are prepared to condemn a man on that and will make no effort to prevent him from being condemned. You do not think of how he might suffer or his family. You only think that you do not wish your name or that of your daughter connected with the affair. You do not care whether he receives justice or not. You are only concerned with your position and with mine, and the fact that being in the affair might reflect badly on your name and my reputation. I don't care a damn about my reputation or what people will say of me [gap in letter] I only feel that if an injustice is being done to a person, and I believe it is, and if I can help to clear up that injustice that I ought. It is no excuse that you won't let me. You have made it impossible for me to be a witness, so in case this is used to discredit myself or Professor Orr, I have written the following—that you won't let me say anything because you are afraid I will reveal that Mr Binns told you what he did. I have sealed it and no one will read it unless I say, or unless my absence in the event of a law case were used to discredit Professor Orr.

As he read further his surprise escalated into fear. He couldn't have imagined anything worse: the silly girl had gone and put the actionable story in writing. Tearing the letter in pieces, he threw it into the fireplace in a rage, before rounding on Suzanne to demand she retrieve the offending statement and destroy it. Suzanne, alarmed by her father's reaction and sensing the invidious position he was now in, agreed to get the statement back within the next few days. Henceforth, her father firmly insisted, the matter of Professor Orr was closed.

Reginald Kemp saw the world in clear-cut terms and he expected his children to do as he told them; no questions asked. It was not such an easy matter for Suzanne to consider the matter closed. She was desperately worried about the possibility of writs, while at the same time tormented by her obligation to stand up for Orr. For several days she fretted and stewed, making no attempt to contact Malcolm Hills or to visit the Orr house. She was hugely relieved when her brother Andrew came home from Burnie for the weekend and she had someone to talk to. In desperation she left a hasty note on his bed; 'Thank God you have come. I need to talk to you. You can help me decide, although I have already decided.'

She was still at her wits' end when Geoffrey Allison called during the weekend. He knew it was time for some straight talking as soon as he saw how upset she was. After Sunday lunch he tackled her directly, telling her that her perception of the world was badly flawed; that her ideas on life and how to deal with it were not valid. Someone had filled her head with a lot of wrong ideas which were in conflict with her basic instincts. And was that someone Professor Orr? Geoffrey wanted to know. Again Suzanne seemed relieved he had asked. She agreed the married man in her life was Sydney Orr. As well she agreed that she needed to talk to her mother and father about this affair.

The Kemp family was fairly typical of middle-class Australia in the 1950s. Theirs was a suburban existence of close-knit domesticity. Weekends were times for the family to be together, as were holidays. Reginald Kemp, while a prosperous and influential businessman had no involvements with the politics or committees which took up so much time of some of his business colleagues. He spent the weekends at home with his family as a matter of course, and Sunday was traditionally a day for quiet relaxation after the Sunday roast. With the unpleasant row with

Suzanne earlier in the week now resolved, Mr and Mrs Kemp could reasonably have expected that Suzanne had no more nasty shocks in store as they sat reading in their lounge room on Sunday 26 February. They were quite unprepared when she approached them, wraith-pale, around six o'clock with a barely coherent story about Professor Orr. In essence she told her parents that what she had said about herself and Professor Orr was untrue. She said that she was in love with Orr, that he believed in free love and that they were lovers and had been for many months. Professor Orr had taught her to see that love was above conventional morality; that it was the supreme value in life. In later evidence Reginald Kemp had difficulty remembering the exact nature of his daughter's confession, it came as such a shock. As for Suzanne, she was in a terrible state. 'If I had not known it was impossible,' he said, 'I would have thought she was drugged ... I have never known her in that condition before.'

Geoffrey Allison had tactfully gone home at teatime, but he returned after six to find Mr and Mrs Kemp sunk in the lounge chairs in a state of shock and confusion. He confirmed Suzanne's story and sat down to discuss what on earth they should do about it. Reginald Kemp was all for confronting Orr, and Allison agreed to accompany him to Hamilton Street. Professor Orr answered the door to the seething father and his young companion and saw them into the front room. Realising something serious was brewing, he sent his wife out to take the two young children off to bed. Turning back to his guests he met a barrage of abuse. Kemp told him he was a lowdown bastard then flung out a fist which landed on the side of Orr's head, sending him tumbling against the wall. He slid down the wall till he rested on the floor while Kemp continued to hit his head and face with an open hand. Allison, on the far side of the room, studied the mantelpiece.

This battering was terminated by the return of a distraught Mrs Orr. Kemp regained his self-control sufficiently to allow the professor to pull himself off the floor, put on a jacket and sit as calmly as possible on the arm of one of the chairs. Orr wanted to know of what he was accused. Reginald Kemp's tenuous self-control slipped one more time as he exploded that Orr damn well knew what it was all about. But no, Professor Orr insisted that he had not the slightest idea, so Kemp repeated Suzanne's story of seduction. It was denied. Reginald Kemp had no intention of pursuing the ins and outs of the rotten business, but with Mrs Orr in the doorway he accepted Geoffrey Allison's suggestion that they listen to what Orr had to say for himself. They each drew up chairs on either side of the fireplace and sat down facing the professor.

In less than measured terms Orr began a long discourse which Geoffrey remembered as 'telling us virtually what he thought of us'. Reginald Kemp was a brute, he declared, as his actions had just shown. It was this brutishness which had destroyed his daughter and reduced her to a psychological case bordering on schizophrenia. He had been treating Suzanne for mental problems for some time and had recommended she see a psychiatrist. Her home life was completely unnatural, with her living in mortal fear of her father who had mistreated her as a child. Both Kemp and Allison remembered Orr insisting that Suzanne was so frightened of her father that she was unable to resist his sexual advances. At this suggestion, and Orr's repeated references to psychological problems, Reginald Kemp grew apoplectic, asserting that Orr had no right to treat his daughter. Orr claimed that Kemp himself was a psychological case, and Allison as well. Repeatedly Orr asked them to consider why Suzanne would say these things: 'Does she say she loves me, or does she imagine she loves me?' Since Kemp could give no rational answer Orr told him that Suzanne would say anything; she was deranged and did not know what she was saying. He further suggested that Suzanne was immoral, claiming she had had sex with at least seven men, including Allison, who said later 'he said he had plenty about her father and myself, that he knew plenty'.

After almost an hour of increasingly wild assertions from

Orr, Reginald Kemp had heard more than enough. As he and Allison made their way out of the house Orr left no doubt that writs for assault and defamation would be laid the very next day; that he had evidence which would disprove the allegation and show that he was being framed by a conspiracy orchestrated by the vice-chancellor. The cornerstone of Orr's threat of retaliation was the written statement from Suzanne. 'That will sound good in court,' he called after them.

Reginald Kemp was in a real pickle. He faced serious charges from his impetuous confrontation with Orr and he believed his daughter was now exposed to blackmail. A late-night dash to Malcolm Hill's home proved fruitless, as Suzanne's statement was in the hands of Orr's legal advisor. There was nothing for it, so Reginald Kemp reasoned, but to go to the university authorities. While this could involve damaging publicity it was hard to see how the sordid affair could be kept out of the public arena with court cases threatening. He didn't want to see his daughter's name dragged through the mud, but he felt strongly that he had an obligation to the university, and its student population, to expose Orr's immorality.

Warren Carey, chairman of the professorial board, was astounded on the morning of 27 February when Geoffrey Allison approached him to complain that a professor had seduced 'his fiancee'. He took Allison's complaint to the vice-chancellor, Torleiv Hytten, who wanted to know if Mr Kemp had requested Allison to approach the university. Reluctantly Professor Carey made an appointment to speak with the Kemp family. In a 'most unpleasant lunch' with Allison, Suzanne, Mr and Mrs Kemp and their solicitor, Reginald Kemp made it clear he wanted the university to sack Orr. When the lunch concluded, Carey spoke at length and in private to Suzanne. 'I had no doubt she was telling the truth about repeated sexual intercourse over several months,' he later wrote. 'The spontaneous detail, her embarrassed frankness and general demeanour were inconsistent with fabrication.'[1]

Returning to the outraged father, Carey made it clear that the university could take no action without Suzanne acting as a material witness in an inquiry into the charge. The family solicitor and Carey both advised the matter be left, to avoid pain and embarrassment to the family. The vice-chancellor, when informed of this advice, did not concur. He phoned Kemp and encouraged him to submit a written complaint to the council meeting on the following Friday, 2 March.

At first Suzanne was horrified by the suggestion. Only a week earlier she had been writing a passionate defence of Orr and his propriety. Now her father wanted her to tell the university council she had been seduced by Orr. She was a ferment of conflicting emotions. However, one aspect of her situation detached itself from the welter to impress itself upon her mind. Sydney had not stood up to her father as a champion of the free expression of human feeling. He had not defended love as the supreme good. Instead he had said that she was psychologically disturbed; that she was making up a relationship between them; that she was immoral in relationships with other men. It was the time-honoured defence of the accused man, but not what she would have expected from Sydney Sparkes Orr. He was not all the man she had believed him to be.

Reluctantly she agreed that her father should make a formal complaint that she had been seduced by Professor Orr, that he had influenced her to make untrue statements about him and that she had been completely under his influence. 'He is mad,' is what she said, 'and I was too.'[2]

CHAPTER TWO

Even if he were guilty ... he was framed

It seems to me that the Orr case has always been part of my life. I remember how his name seeped through the walls at the parties my parents held in our big timber house on the mountain above Hobart, when I was not yet ten. I would often sneak out of bed and sit in the hallway to catch glimpses of women in taffeta or satin, and catch snatches of loosened talk and rowdy laughter. In retrospect, the rights and wrongs of the Orr case were always in the mix somewhere. Hobart society fed on it. Everyone had taken sides. What else was there to talk about?

My family left Hobart and its internecine drama in 1957 so this, like so much else of that small world, was cast aside. Well, not entirely so, since the Orr case pursued us to the cities of the mainland. For my parents, seeking a toehold in the intellectual smalltalk of their new environment, the Orr case was something they knew about; something special they might contribute. It was not until 1965 that I heard their story with any kind of clarity. Our neighbour, a promising young academic, had thought to apply for a position at the University of Tasmania. To his consternation he had been informed by colleagues that the staff association had a black ban on positions at that university, and should he apply he would never get another job in an Australian university. He was indignant: such draconian restrictions were monstrous.

My parents explained to him how ten years earlier, Sydney Sparkes Orr, a radical professor of philosophy had made quite a name for himself as a vocal critic of the Tasmanian establishment. His public criticisms led to a royal commission into the university in 1955, which was critical of the council and the chancellor. Within months of that finding, early in 1956, a prominent Hobart businessman and powerbroker had made a complaint to the university council that Professor Orr had seduced his daughter. Orr was summarily dismissed without due process by the council, acting on her uncorroborated story. The girl's evidence was totally suspect, they insisted, and she was clearly being used to get rid of Orr, who was deemed a troublemaker. Such things happen in a small, conservative and closed society, was the message. The girl had later married a tutor at the university who had been one of Orr's accusers and who had been rewarded with a job on the campus. Orr, protesting his innocence and insisting the girl had invented the whole thing, had fought to have his name cleared and to obtain compensation from the university. Since 1960 he had been supported by the Federal Council of University Staff Associations (FCUSA) which had imposed the ban on the university which now so concerned our friend, and the Australian Association of Philosophers had succeeded in enforcing a worldwide ban on the chair, which had not been filled since Orr's departure in 1956. My parents were not sanguine about the future for their home state's only university. Our neighbour decided he would apply for a less attractive, but unimpeded, position elsewhere.

Of course this telling was spiced with delicious embellishment about players in the drama who were known, whose foibles, or worse, could be authenticated with anecdotes. It was this sense of intimacy with events that most impressed me, and that I was able to adopt at Sydney University where I found myself amongst a good many ardent Orr supporters. Like so many other aspiring bohemians I had made a beeline for the Newcastle Hotel (or Jim Buckley's as it was known by the *cognoscenti*), where the Sydney libertarian push liked to drink and talk, crammed shoulder to shoulder every Friday evening. Orr was an occasional topic of conversation, I was thrilled to discover, and I had inside information to share. Among this gathering of intellectuals—lecturers, wharfies, lawyers, gamblers and journalists—one felt the dominant presence of the late and immoderately revered Professor John Anderson. He, along with his colleague Professor Alan Stout, had first raised the alarm about Orr's dismissal in 1957. Unlike Professor Stout, with his cautious emphasis on proper procedures, Anderson has been of the opinion, the sort of opinion for which he was revered, that it was not the business of university authorities what a lecturer and student might do out of the tutorial room: 'Students are not children,' was his line, 'and the personal relationships of either staff or students are not the universities' concern.'[3] In this he was enthusiastically supported by younger men, with whom I found myself drinking. One of these young turks, perhaps the most attractive to my eager eye, was George Molnar, who had little time for Orr because he refused to take a principled stand on sexual freedom, preferring to side with 'the sexually repressive morality of his opponents'. As far as Molnar could see, the pro-Orr and anti-Orr champions had enough in common for people like himself, advocates of sexual freedom, 'to wish a plague on both their houses'.[4]

Not just the libertarians but other left-liberal academics wondered why so few people had asked the obvious question: does it matter? In *Overland*, Ian Turner stated his opinion: 'If so, so what?' Even the radical Catholic, Bill Ginnane, undoubtedly Orr's staunchest advocate, was on record in *Prospect* as saying that the question of Orr's guilt was irrelevant: 'Even if he were guilty ... he was framed.' The general tenor of opinion around the bar was that it was not on to strip a man of his career over a dalliance, and that it was clear Orr had been 'done' by the University of Tasmania which had manifestly failed to accord him natural justice. The fact that support for the university came from such ideological enemies as James McAuley and the *Quadrant* bunch made support of Orr so much easier. Even those who were sick to death of the case, which had absorbed so much staff association business time at Sydney University for so long, were inclined to admit that something fishy had gone on in Hobart.

The man who was the real expert on the case was the redoubtable Harry Eddy, the senior tutor in the adult education extension at Sydney University, whom I would encounter at parties and adult education courses for which my friends were tutors. He was an odd sort of fellow to my eye, and hardly one to set the world on fire. The case had completely captivated him and in 1961 he had published a monumental study, entitled simply *Orr*. It was Eddy's detailed analysis to which anyone discussing the case referred and by which, it seemed, they were entirely convinced. His advocacy had raised Orr to the status of *cause célèbre* and invited comparisons with Dreyfus. According to an academic reviewing the book in the *Cambridge Review*, Orr was 'the Dreyfus of our times', a refrain echoed by academics in the USA, Canada, New Zealand and Australia (although not in Tasmania). Eddy would have none of the libertarians' generosity toward sex between lecturers and their students. The essential feature of the Orr case, he insisted, was Orr's innocence of the accusation of seduction. The professor had been tried by a star chamber, which had denied him any semblance of natural justice. In his interpretation there was no doubt that Orr was framed, that evidence against him was cynically and ruthlessly concocted and that he was being destroyed because he had exposed the university to the humiliation of the royal commission.

As well as comparing the case to that of Dreyfus, Eddy drew a powerful parallel between Sydney Sparkes Orr and the seventeenth-century Leveller John Lilburne. But where 'Free born John' had been judged by his peers, and found not guilty, Orr, denied peer judgement, was 'defamed, deprived of his means of livelihood and reduced to a position close to outlawry'. Compared to the university council in 1956, some three hundred years earlier 'Cromwell's government went about its attack on Lilburne like a comparatively honest Tyranny.' Without making direct comparisons with twentieth-century repressions, Eddy implied that connections were to be made, concluding: 'I do not know any case in a democratic country where this kind of thing has been done on the same scale, or as systematically, as in the Orr case.'

Eddy's exposé of what he saw as the deliberate victimisation of Orr was hard-hitting and generally people who read it were shocked. As far afield as North America, a Professor Murdock, writing in the journal of the American Association of University Professors, posed the question: 'What causes university men to act in such a way toward a colleague ... was it horror at the idea of sexual relations between professor and student, or was it the fear of a man of strength who was unwilling to compromise on questions of academic freedom and self-government, one who was willing to fight for his ideals at all risks?' In Australia, intellectuals of the left, and not just in Sydney, took up Eddy's theme. Historian Brian Fitzpatrick titled his lengthy *Meanjin* review 'An Injustice has been Done', claiming Eddy's work had 'the stamp of truth, of utter conviction—the overwhelming verisimilitude of Zola's *J'Accuse*,' and he found an obvious parallel with the IWW members sentenced to long prison terms for political activity in 1916.

Bill Ginnane began his review in *Prospect* with rhetorical hype: 'Evil is nowhere more terrible than when it penetrates high places and clothes itself in the protective garb of legal sanction and institutional prestige'. Warming to the theme he wrote of the 'malice, deceit and treachery with which charges against Orr were gradually concocted' and how 'person after person became ensnared in the web of fear and malice.' This was not simply a miscarriage of justice but 'the symptomatic corruption of an institution by its own government' and born out of a community 'presided over by a power elite clinging to its position by legal subterfuge'. By no means everyone was convinced: in the *Sydney Morning Herald*, Angus Maude found the book 'inspires no great confidence in Mr. Eddy's motives or methods,' while Donald Horne, in the *Bulletin*, was equally unimpressed. In the libertarian and left-wing world to which I aspired, such doubters were easily dismissed as lackeys of the capitalist press or agents of right-wing subterfuge. As Bill Ginnane claimed, such responses were calculated to 'assist in the putrefaction of Australian life'.

Whatever the enthusiasm of some in the libertarian left, by the time I arrived at the campus of Sydney University in 1965 it was apparent that most academics were fed up with the Orr case and wanted the matter closed. A curious eighty-five page booklet, published by the Association of Philosophers in June the previous year and known as 'the yellow book', was still in circulation; it argued, somewhat incoherently, for continued support for Orr. In his own defence, an appendix of fifty-eight pages, Orr reiterated his innocence and eight-year struggle to 'have my name cleared and a grave misjustice put right'. In so doing he considered himself engaged in a crusade for all academics: 'if one of us can be dismissed on false allegations, with no redress, then the same thing can happen to any other academic.'[5] Nevertheless, during 1965 the will to continue the war of attrition against the University of Tasmania ebbed. The censure notice disappeared from the pages of the FCUSA journal *Vestes* and in early 1966 a special meeting was held at which it was agreed that academics taking positions at the University of Tasmania would no longer face censure from the organisation. The Association of Philosophers, it was rumoured, was about to follow suit in lifting its ban on the chair of philosophy.

The increasingly isolated Orr seemed determined to fight on, so it was a surprise when national newspapers announced on 7 May 1966 that ex-Professor Orr had finally accepted a cash payment of $32 000 in return for withdrawing his legal actions. The Orr case, to everyone's great relief, was finally over. Among my associates at Sydney, there was some concern that nothing had been done to secure him another academic job and on 25 June the *Australian* reported claims that Orr was being kept out of universities by a whisper campaign. I knew differently. I knew from family friends visiting the Royal Hobart Hospital that Orr was gravely ill and that this was probably why he had accepted a settlement. He died on 16 July 1966.

In his obituary, Harry Eddy recalled Orr's moral courage and utter dedication to his cause: 'It must be six years ago that he said to me "The forces arrayed against me are probably too powerful for me to win an overt and decisive victory. What is important is for me to keep on struggling as long as I have the strength to do it".' To the end Orr maintained his total innocence, declaring to an old adversary on his deathbed 'I swear to you I never laid a finger on that girl.'[6]

Orr's status as a victim of repressive systems was assured. His case had become absorbed into the intellectual mythology of the nation, as the academy's own martyr to be invoked whenever university authorities flexed their muscle or academic colleagues were threatened. I was able to parly my knowledge of the case into the occasional discussion of Orr over the next two decades, and this was the one dominant relic of my Tasmanian past I still had intact when I returned there to live in 1985.

Finding myself employed at the University of Tasmania I immediately set about establishing a reputation for gaucherie by asking direct questions about Orr. I met a somewhat frosty response: 'Oh that's all in the past,' some would airily say, and nothing more. Others were more pointed: 'We do not talk about the Orr case in Tasmania.' I could see that sensibilities were still bruised, that some wounds would never heal. Those who had lived through the internecine trauma of 1956–66 were justifiably anxious that the lid be kept on those long-dormant angers and resentments. Yet I could see that the Orr case simmered away just below the surface and was far from resolved. People were too guarded, too defensive and too obviously pained by my interest.

I had also discovered, and plunged into, that other internecine maelstrom—environmental politics. About eighteen months later, as a direct result of my political involvement in 'green' issues, I found my own situation resembling Professor Orr's in uncomfortable ways. My husband and myself were abruptly sacked as joint managers of the university research company following complaints about our political activity from powerful business interests in the state. We can't say we weren't warned that was how business was done in Robin Gray's state, we were just naive in thinking it didn't apply to the university. Unlike Orr's, this case was resolved smartly and amicably thanks to the immediate and whole-hearted intervention of the staff association.

My own case attracted some notoriety, mercifully brief, as a result of which I received a review copy of a book entitled *Intellectual Suppression*, edited by Brian Martin and others. It was a series of case studies of intellectual suppression and, not surprisingly, the spectre of Orr pervaded the enterprise. I was surprised to see that the case history of Professor Orr, 'Not Merely Malice', was written by academics unconnected with the original case. All the better for objectivity, I felt, although I was a bit taken aback by the opening quote from Orr: 'I must confess to a feeling of panic, a kind of fear such as I had never known even in war-time, during the blitzes, the fear of being without protection of the law; and for the first time I realized something of what it must be like to fall foul of authorities in a totalitarian regime.' Reiterating the opinion that Orr was convicted on 'evidence that would not hang a dog', the authors, Clyde Manwell and CM Ann Baker, relied almost solely on Harry Eddy's account, especially in describing those 'techniques of totalitarianism' which were used against Orr to alienate support from his colleagues. For the first time I became aware that there had been three other accusations of academic impropriety against Orr from students and colleagues, mentioned in the essay only to 'show how easily some staff members will join a campaign once they perceive there is powerful support from higher authority.' In conclusion the authors pulled no punches: 'Orr is dead but the issues live. The problem is not just the abuse of administrative power. That abuse requires compliance. It is not merely the malice of power-seeking personalities. It is the ability of certain intellectuals to rationalise any injustice as long as their own pursuit of glory or comfort is not disturbed.'

There was something so immoderate, so holier-than-thou, in this that it gave me pause. After all, I had talked to academics involved in the case and, however reticent or defensive they might have been, there was no sense that they had been cravenly co-opted into Orr's victimisation. The issues were much more complex; that much I knew. The time had finally come to read that great tome of Harry Eddy's for myself. Mind you, finding it wasn't easy. Although at the time it was published the *Bulletin* reported hot sales in Tasmania, there were none on the shelves of the public library, nor the university library. In time I did secure a copy and settled down to plough my way through it—no mean feat, as it happened, since the outstanding feature of *Orr* is its impenetrability.

After the first confusing, overwrought and turgid chapters I had good reason to suppose that few people had actually read this book and that its author's claim to objectivity was a nonsense. The wildly partisan and extremist tone annoyed me, but did not deflect my interest: we were on the same side, so to speak. Again I noted those serious allegations against Orr from his colleagues and a mature male student; allegations made *before* the allegations from Suzanne Kemp. But what drew me up short with astonishment was a letter published in full from Suzanne Kemp to Professor Orr written from her holiday house at Orford. In the subsequent Supreme Court case the judge had considered this a critical piece of evidence. 'It is a remarkable document,' he said in his judgement. Indeed it is. Eddy spent a lengthy chapter trying to establish that this letter was proof of an hysterical imagination (if she wrote it at all), which to me indicated that he knew nothing of the psychology of women or the techniques of textual analysis; for if Suzanne had concocted this letter for the purposes of trapping Professor Orr, she has missed out on a promising career as a novelist, such is the verisimilitude of the piece.

Having read and re-read the letter, I find it has several elements. First there is the typical teasing of a lover who is away and wants to engender just enough anxiety in her love to keep him on his toes in case his attention should wander. And for an older man what could be more piquant than a much younger suitor, serious-minded and intelligent to boot: 'I guess you want to hear about Geoff's stay,' she writes, obliging with an exaggerated account of his suit and the fascination she holds for him: 'The position is serious, at least for him ... have I allowed a situation to develop I'm not prepared to handle ... he tried in a timid way making love to me.' Reassuringly, she insists this was rebuffed. So the picture she paints is of her toying with the desperate affections of a callow youth, while registering with a shrug of the shoulders that her lover is 'neglected and forgotten'. It's a time-honoured game of absent lovers.

But Geoffrey Allison's visit is also used to illuminate the overwhelming sense of doubt and confusion which quite immobilises Suzanne. This strange condition she superficially attributes to toothache, but hastens to add that Geoff 'thought it was something far deeper than that'. Her own shifting references suggest that she does too. She describes a state of mind which is more than romantic vagueness or ennui: 'Escaping is becoming a mania with me.' What she seems to need to escape is not the timid attentions of Geoffrey Allison but the dominating lover who acts as critic, teacher and interrogator whom she appears to have completely internalised. 'You haunted me in fiendish forms,' she says, and elsewhere: 'your outlook on life and mine in me have become so mixed I cannot separate them.'

The questions she continually poses suggest his voice, probing, pushing, criticising, scolding, reproving. But Suzanne does have gumption. She tries to resist. The dominant idea 'that love is supreme and good' does not convince her in the face of realities of love's disappointments. As for the other notion that one cannot love unless it is returned, this too she resists with touching ambivalence: 'I know how much you are sustained by love and it rather frightens me. It gives me so much power,' she naively asserts against all the evidence of her letter to the contrary. She does make a valiant try to assert her own core of being as inviolable and intact: 'You have not that power over me, or not so much ... you haven't touched my very being, even though you are the centre of my life. Maybe no one ever will. Maybe I would never give it.' It's a plucky try, but almost immediately the internalised interrogator appears, suggesting this is 'only my childish streak coming through to hurt'. Furthermore she anticipates that he will bring in his armoury of psychological warfare to deal with her aberration.

Suzanne's confused attempts to assert her inviolate self against the almost omnipotent power of her lover—'Perhaps unconsciously you and He have swapped places in my mind'—is the key element in the letter to which all the other elements refer. What she tells him is that she still has her untouched central core; that there is a nice, intelligent boy who desires her; that she belongs in a community, however dull, where 'for once, thank goodness, I am not an outsider.'

It is a letter full of passion and ambivalence, redolent with adolescent introspection, as well as genuine confusion. In short it is, as Sir Kenneth Green, said in his Supreme Court summation, 'exactly the kind of letter a girl might write at the stage of a relationship that Miss Kemp had reached with Professor Orr'. Now around the bar of Jim Buckley's, and intellectual discussions in Sydney, this was neither here nor there. Everyone knew that some academics had affairs with impressionable students, and you certainly wouldn't ruin a man for it. But Orr insisted, and Eddy reiterated emphatically, he had not had an affair; her accusation was concocted as part of a conspiracy to destroy him. On the basis of this defence they had mounted a sustained attack on the credibility of Suzanne Kemp's evidence and her motives; an attack which continued, from what I had recently read, unabated.

I read Suzanne's letter to my mother. She was at first astonished. 'I never heard about this before,' she said. There was much more, I told her, 'the girl kept a diary which is remarkably revealing.' The next day my mother was visibly upset. She had been a vocal feminist for many years, she had also been a mature-age university student and so knew first-hand about dalliances between staff and students, yet Suzanne Kemp's perfidy had remained an article of faith with her for all these years. While her views on so many matters had been reviewed and recast, the Orr case had remain frozen in the fixed partisan attitude of the time. Then she had not examined the issues closely but accepted, in her distaste for the insular, conservative mentality of Hobart, that Orr had been framed. In turn I had inherited her uncritical, partisan point of view. The time had come to give the matter some close scrutiny.

CHAPTER THREE

Just a bloody nuisance

Who was Sydney Sparkes Orr? He was born on 16 December 1914, the son of Telford and Elizabeth Orr of Annsborough, County Down in Northern Ireland. As a child he appears to have been a bit of an outsider, suffering from a congenital heart defect which limited his involvement with other children. This may have contributed to his belief that he was different. Perhaps too it helped foster the introspection and self-absorption which at some point convinced him that he was illegitimate, so that in his later life he would be tormented by not knowing who had been his father.

In the years 1936–39 he completed his undergraduate degree at Queen's University, Belfast, graduating with first-class honours in philosophy. He was awarded an MA in philosophy in 1941. In that year, after nine years of courtship, he married Sarah, a fair-haired country girl he had met through church activities. During 1942–45 he was engaged in research on 'The Socratic doctrine that virtue is knowledge' for a doctorate of philosophy. This degree was never awarded.

In 1944 he was appointed as a temporary assistant lecturer at St Andrews University in Scotland, lecturing in the department of logic and metaphysics, with an understanding that the following year a grade three lectureship would be confirmed. This was normal practice at Scottish universities. To his great disappointment, Orr found the position no longer available to him at the end of the academic year. The official reason given was the return of servicemen who were members of staff, but the correspondence makes abundantly clear that this was not the real reason.

Certainly Orr was not prepared to take the reason for the termination of his teaching at face value, protesting vigorously at the breach of understanding about the job. Although the department head, Professor JN Wright, had originally supported Orr and given him a reference for a job in New Zealand, by July 1945 he was refusing to write a job recommendation for Orr, suggesting that his examiners at Queen's, Professor Selincourt and Professor Macbeath, would be better referees.[7] The response of Professor Macbeath was that he 'was not prepared to support him for any post nor act as referee'.[8] Nor was a reference forthcoming from Selincourt.

After five months on unemployment benefits Orr was pretty desperate and wrote to the principal of St Andrews requesting an explanation as to why the position he had occupied still remained vacant while he was still in St Andrews and unemployed. On the same day the head of the Presbyterian College at Belfast wrote to the principal:

> It is difficult for me to understand what happened at St Andrews, and, with my knowledge of Mr Orr, I am inclined to think an injustice has been done, perhaps unwittingly, by the termination of his work there ... I have reason to believe that statements about him which are inaccurate or prejudiced or based on misrepresentation of incidents, have been made and these should be scrutinized with care ... I am especially sorry about Mr Orr having this time of strain when doctors definitely desire for him to have peace and quiet on medical grounds.[9]

Judging by another letter of support for Orr, sent some months earlier by Greek scholar Jonathon Tate, Professor Macbeath had 'condemned in the most forthright terms Orr, his work, his character and his aspirations to a permanent post in Philosophy'.[10] In later years, Macbeath made it clear that his concern stemmed from Orr's poor scholarship (he had twice rejected the PhD thesis) and his improper relationships with his students. Just what these improper relationships might have been is anyone's guess, but Macbeath spoke of Orr psychoanalysing female students in his university room at Belfast. Not that Macbeath's poor opinion would have turned the tide against Orr, since Professor Wright, it is apparent, had developed his own poor opinion of his temporary lecturer.

Contemporaries and students of Orr's from St Andrews remember clearly that Orr and Wright did not get on. The professor, a puritanical and patrician figure who kept remote from students, may have taken a dim view of Orr's casual approach. As one ex-students recalls 'it is impossible to imagine Wright, still garbed in cap and gown after service at the university chapel, walking down a St Andrews street with his wife on a Sunday licking ice-cream cornets! As Mr and Mrs Orr did. Even many of his students looked at this askance and thought it a bit infra dig.' It is more likely that the content of Orr's lectures caused Wright annoyance. Lecturing almost exclusively to young women (during the war), Orr's lectures rapidly made a name because

> he always managed to bring sex into them for no good reason we could understand ... Somewhat shattered by the appearance of overtly sexual remarks and content in formal lectures we used to rush back to our residencies ... to say in shocked tones—'Do you know what he said today ...?' As a result his lectures were extremely well attended.[11]

Further, Orr did not believe in following the syllabus, and, as this same student told me, 'one result of his deviation from past teaching had unsettling results for some St Andrews students.' At the university college in Dundee philosophy students took the exam as set by the lecturer from St Andrews. In 1944 however Orr had written an exam paper based on his own unorthodox lectures and failed to consult with the Dundee lecturer about the differences from the set course. 'The shock of Orr's exam to the Dundee students and lecturer had been extreme.'[12] It was after this exam that Orr found his expectations of a permanent post dashed.

There could have been yet another reason for Wright's displeasure. I have been told that a young woman student, whom I will call Miss G, had made assignations with Orr on the golf links. This was common knowledge amongst the student body and, in a small university town, where everyone played golf, the chances are it was known to others as well. Professor Macbeath seems to have known about it, as he remarked some years later upon Orr's moral laxity at St Andrews.

In 1946 Orr was appointed to a temporary vacancy in the philosophy department at Melbourne University, replacing a lecturer on leave. This job was converted into a permanent lectureship in 1947. Amongst his colleagues, Orr was regarded as an old-fashioned, and perhaps pedestrian philosopher—although zealous is a word used often with regard to his approach to his chosen area, the study of Plato. Ex-students recall his lectures as intellectually unremarkable, except that he did not give sufficient attention to the set texts but instead digressed on to pet topics of his own. Bill Joske, then an undergraduate, remembers that Orr was the only lecturer he heard students universally condemn, often quite seriously asserting that 'the man was mad.'[13]

One undergraduate had a vivid memory of her experiences. 'We loathed Orr,' she wrote to me, explaining how she had agreed to tackle him to

> give the lectures we expected from our reading of the handbook rather than raving on about shooting communists from the rooftops ... he was quite outraged at being approached by a student and said in tones of

> astonished indignation 'None of my students at St Andrews (Soont Arrndroos) would have dared speak to me as you do'. We then promenaded outside the arts tower ... I suppose it wasted ten minutes in a one-sided diatribe about what cheeky upstarts Australian students were and a lot about the dangers of the reds ... it was a futile attempt on my part—the fellow seemed hysterical.[14]

Other students have reported that Orr paid particular attention to his young women students, and two women students confirmed that he made overt sexual advances toward them. His unorthodox approach to female students is apparent in this account from Kevin Grover concerning his then girlfriend:

> in her tutorial discussions of concepts like love Orr noticed that she often seemed to be day-dreaming and was finding difficulty in discussing these notions without emotional stress and confusion. Orr suggested after the close of one such tutorial that she come to his office to talk about the problem ... that he had correctly surmised was her developing relationship with me. She told me that this personal counselling and its intimacy had come as a surprise to her, but that Orr had not sought to exploit the opportunity for sexual advances or suggestions on his part.[15]

Generally the undergraduate women were not impressed with this diminutive, chain-smoking and unprepossessing man, with his receding hair, thin face and self-obsessed babble. He found a more receptive audience at the two adult education courses he taught and the lectures on philosophy of religion he gave for the College of Divinity. Among the Student Christian Movement he also enjoyed high esteem, with his implacable opposition to logical positivism and to communism. Those who liked Orr were drawn by his Irish intensity and his radical brand of Christian theology, which drew on his absorption with the Platonic concept of love. He felt that he had a mission to redeem the world through love. It was a persuasive line for some, who found the little Irishman a dynamic and charismatic lay preacher. In full rhetorical flight Orr was able to transcend his stooped and insignificant body and hold his audience by the power of his glittering eyes. Almost without exception, everyone who encountered Orr was struck by the intensity of his eyes.

I cannot determine at what point, or for what reason, Orr incurred the displeasure of his departmental head, Alexander Boyce Gibson. Contemporaries report that Orr was incensed at not being given a senior lectureship in 1949 and that a confrontation occurred between him and Boyce Gibson which verged on violence. Gibson was also a Plato scholar and was known to have a low opinion of Orr's 'emotional' interpretation of Plato. Whatever the reason, it seems that Gibson came to regard Orr with a lasting enmity which was quite uncharacteristic. One colleague remarked on the intensity of feeling nearly a decade later: 'people don't normally go on hating that long, and Gibson in such cases usually tries to be charitable to his enemies.'[16]

Certainly the dislike was not apparent in the references Gibson gave Orr. In 1948 he gave Orr strong support for the chair at Otago, writing: 'He has thrown himself zealously into the life of the department and shown an intelligent interest in how a department works ... he is keen and zealous in everything he undertakes.' Orr's academic work on Plato was 'well advanced and requires for completion only a concentrated spurt'. Much the same sentiments recurred in the 1950 application for the chair at Adelaide, when Gibson 'greatly looked forward to the completion of his present study'. In late 1951 he wrote again, in support of the application for Tasmania, reiterating Orr's enthusiasm and devotion to his subject, but sounding a little weary about the work on Plato, which was said to be 'undergoing final revision and expected to be ready for publication in the near future'. Gibson might well look eagerly toward the completion of this opus, since Orr had published almost nothing during his tenure at Melbourne.[17]

It was during the time in Melbourne that Orr conceived the notion that he was the illegitimate son of Edward VIII, later the Duke of Windsor. There is no doubt that his stoop and his profile did show a resemblance to the Duke of Windsor, as he was in the habit of pointing out to friends and colleagues. There were some on the staff at Melbourne who felt he was 'an unbalanced personality'.[18] Professor Boyce Gibson may have been one of these. One thing that contemporaries are quite sure about is that the professor, and especially his strong-minded wife Katie, greatly disapproved of Orr's unusual domestic arrangements.

Orr arrived in Melbourne alone and was joined by his wife several months later. In the interim Orr had met a young woman, to be referred to as A, at a Student Christian Movement conference. A was a striking and forthright brunette from a very well-known and well-placed family in Sydney. She was twenty-one and a social worker, not a student. Orr was attracted by her considerable intelligence and her challenge to conventional theology and they formed an intense relationship which was both spiritual and sexual. When Sadie Orr arrived from Ireland she found herself alone in a strange country, with no relatives or friends, landed with an emotional crisis. 'I suppose I could have walked out,' she told a Hobart court years later, 'but I wished to preserve my marriage.' It was Sadie who invited A to live with Orr as another wife: 'She would never have come to live with us otherwise.' All agreed that they would live together in a marriage which was bound by the higher ideals of love and not mere conventional morality. To symbolise the sanctity of their unconventional union, the three had a wedding ceremony which bound them to each other.

As Orr expounded in a series of articles he wrote for *Pix* between June and July 1957, their relationship had its ups and downs, like all marriages, but there was a strong attachment between the women, with A nursing Mrs Orr through a difficult pregnancy. 'There was at all times much to wonder at in the attitude of trust, affection and understanding between them,' he wrote.

> If I were to indicate the finest moments, the noblest achievements of our love, the most exquisite experience in the relationship between us three I would say it was the many happy hours we spent together in mutual appreciation of ... a little child ... I can only bear witness to the fact that was the noblest and most unsullied, the tenderest and most beautiful thing I had ever beheld on earth, or hope to catch sight of this side of heaven.

Orr believed that his colleagues in Melbourne understood A to be merely a close family friend. 'At times,' he says, 'what would they have thought had they known the friendship between us ... was love which according to one eminent theologian is friendship at its best.' Well, they did know, and in contrast to Orr's beatific account of their magnanimous response, generally regarded the ménage as a minor scandal—or they were just incredulous, as was one academic who, when told of the relationship by A, 'presumed she was having romantic delusions'.[19] In contrast too is the account of the affair A herself gave to the Bishop of Tasmania after she had fled from the Orr household with her newborn child in 1951.

Why am I telling you this salacious detail? Believe me, it is all relevant, since, unhappily, all of this experiment in human relationships became subject to public scrutiny after 1956.

While it could be said that the account given in these letters was exaggerated and influenced by emotional disappointment, I found that she was able to confirm the picture when I met her thirty years after she last saw Orr. She impressed me with her calm, intelligent and sympathetic assessment of the man she had loved, perhaps still loved, which matched in many particulars those I had independently uncovered. In A's view Orr was a disturbed and tragic man, charismatic and persuasive for all that. She described herself as having been 'influenced in the most extraordinary way, almost as if hypnotised and yet doubtful and confused and warring' within herself. A insisted that Orr believed himself to be 'especially gifted in his love and knowledge of truth,' a love which he 'equated and indeed identified with the love of God.' Looking to explain her own long involvement with this deluded man, A gave this account: 'he has an extraordinary power over people (of which I was obviously one), being able to do and say what is against their own will. He will go to any length and use any means he thinks will be successful in gaining his own ends ... his own self-glorification and self-justification.'

Initially A had found him charming and interesting when he would 'talk about all the wonderful and beautiful ideals of his life in an almost intoxicating way ... he can make an untruth sound so wonderful that one seeks to pursue it.' But in the domestic sphere she found a troubled and insecure man who would fly into rages and subject her to psychological and physical violence. It is her view that the closeness between herself and Sadie Orr sprang from the mutual protection they gave each other. On one occasion she vividly recalled she had to restrain him from actually going to Professor Boyce Gibson's house to 'do for him'. A also gives a disturbing picture of a man with a powerful sexual drive who consistently sought out young women students. 'He went too far with at least two girls to my knowledge' in Melbourne and had told her, and his wife, about his conquests at St Andrews. She came to understand that Orr was dangerously deluded and compulsive and, using her own contacts in the profession, had persuaded Orr to seek psychiatric help. During 1951 he was the patient of a leading Melbourne psychiatrist.

A finally made a break with Orr after she found herself pregnant in August 1950. Orr, to her shock, reacted with what she felt was gross hypocrisy, insisting that she live apart from him and his wife until the child was born. His concern, she believed, was the conventional fear of scandal. Nevertheless, A did move into a boarding-house in St Kilda and, following the child's birth she returned to her family in Sydney, abruptly cutting all her ties with Orr. Both Orr and his wife tried desperately to get her to return; Sadie in particular writing pleading letters about Orr's despair. A was determined to separate for the sake of her new child. It was greatly distressing, but 'it was best for all of us—especially Sadie—so we could get on with a normal life.'[20]

Writing in *Pix* of this traumatic period in his life, Orr said:

> The full horror of what A was doing now began to dawn on me, though not the motive for it ... she knew, though it had never been much discussed, about my own illegitimacy ... I was the father who himself, as a child had been so deprived when equally helpless to do anything about it, and who knew therefore from bitter experience every minute thought and feeling, longing and frustration, conflict and problem his own child would know ... the furies themselves could not have devised a more diabolical trick.

He was convinced that A was under the malign influence of her mother and in need of psychological help. Orr himself was so traumatised that he had to go to hospital for a time due to the strain on his heart.

It was during this very stressful period that Orr applied for the foundation chair of philosophy in Tasmania. He was appointed in the middle of 1952 and left Melbourne for Hobart with his anguish over A and his lost child dominating his days and nights. It was hardly a state of mind conducive to the demands of setting up a new department in a desperately underfunded university. He sought psychological help from the Anglican bishop, Dr Cranswick, who was an old family friend of A's. It was as a result of his intervention in the drama that A wrote her frank and unflattering portrait of Orr. Her purpose, she made quite clear, was not to attack but to show how the best interests of her child and herself lay in disconnection from Orr. As the bishop discovered when he went to see A, 'she experienced strong revulsion to what had happened and was filled with remorse that she had allowed herself to be party to such an arrangement'.[21] Also enlisted in Orr's emotional struggle was an émigré philosopher, Dr Kajica Milanov, who was working as a psychologist in Hobart. Orr asked Milanov, a highly qualified scholar from Yugoslavia, to lecture part-time in his department while also engaging in a lengthy process of psychoanalysis with him. Orr discussed with him a hypothetical relationship between a woman 'from the highest social circles' and a married man and his wife, what he described as 'a three-fold cord relationship'. The woman had left for no apparent or sufficient reason and the man 'at the top of his career' was ruined unless she returned to him. It was apparent to Milanov that Orr was talking about himself, since he raised the case several times when he collected Milanov after lectures to drive him home. He did finally confess one day, when he had driven Milanov to the Domain, weeping emotionally as he did so. Startled, Milanov suggested Orr consult a psychiatrist, since his own knowledge of psychoanalysis was only theoretical. Privately, as a refugee from Nazism and communism, he was disturbed by the reference to 'the highest social circles'. He found Orr's behaviour very worrying and felt that if something went wrong he 'was going to be on the losing side'. Nevertheless Orr was persistent and his lecturer agreed to the psychoanalytic sessions several times a week. Bishop Cranswick was also involved as a co-counsellor. It was apparent to them both that Orr wanted to re-kindle his threefold relationship. He had presented them both with a book by Maud Royden, *The Three Fold Cord*, in which she discussed her platonic love for a famous married cleric. Neither would accept his insistence that the relationship was salvageable and urged him to put it behind him. Milanov was disturbed too by Orr's revelations that he was the illegitimate son of Edward VIII. He tried to disabuse Orr of his delusions about this. 'I told him that a king is only a king if he is on a throne. Being the illegitimate son of a dethroned king has no special value.'[22]

On the advice of Milanov and the bishop, Orr was referred to a psychiatrist from Melbourne. Milanov continued to act as psychoanalyst in Hobart, corresponding with the Melbourne doctor. 'I agree with you that the psychological state of Professor Orr is very difficult,' he wrote in May 1954,

> and maybe you are right that it is grave ... at the bottom of his symptoms are firstly the inferiority complex caused by his being an illegitimate child and not knowing his father and feelings of inferiority caused by a congenital weakness of the heart and body ... a serious duality and internal discordance of soul ... is it any wonder then that he is only happy in his threefold relationship and that he is emotionally so seriously upset by the collapse of his relationship with A because his own personality seems to be bereft of half its foundation.

The Melbourne doctor agreed with Milanov but felt Orr must see a qualified psychiatrist in Hobart. He later explained to Milanov, 'I felt [Orr] needed some watching by a person whom the law accepted as authorized to take this responsibility. If he had gone on and done something stupid your position might have been seriously embarrassing'.[23] Written in May 1954 this observation proved to be remarkably prescient.

Wishing to disentangle himself from Orr's emotional turmoil, Dr Milanov was faced with the complication of having been appointed full-time to the philosophy department very largely as a result of Orr's enthusiastic representations on his behalf. In 1954 Orr could not speak highly enough of his new member of staff, whom he applauded as: 'a man of wide scholarship and outstanding philosophical acumen'.[24] According to some staff and students of the time, Orr also made it quite apparent that he regarded himself as the patron of this timid refugee with his halting English and ever-present anxiety. Milanov was out of place in provincial Hobart, with his memories of the Nazi death camps and the refugee camps of Europe. He had spent three years in a German POW camp and had met his Jewish wife, herself a survivor of Auschwitz, in a displaced persons camp in Austria. They had come to Tasmania in 1949 because it was as far away from the place of their nightmare as they could envisage.

The university campus was not a tranquil place in 1954, however. It was desperately overcrowded, with shabby temporary accommodation spread over three locations. According to Chancellor Sir John Morris in 1944 the university was in 'the dingiest and most repellent condition ... [with] lecture rooms calculated to discourage anyone but a moron.'[25] Plans were made to create a new university on a site at Sandy Bay, but a decade later these had been effectively shelved by the Labor government. By then the university exuded 'an atmosphere of decay and sordidness reminiscent of tenements'.[26] Staff were poorly paid and poorly regarded, with non-academic members of council deriding academic work, contemptuous of research and uninterested in questions of salaries and conditions. For the Labor government, the future for the state lay in industrial expansion built on hydro-electric power, and into this utopian project the state had poured vast sums of public money. To the government, university staff had a strictly utilitarian role in training engineers and clerks. They should not entertain any superior notions about themselves.

Passions were inflamed by October 1954 when the embattled

staff association at the university decided to step up pressure on the government. In this it had no support from the dynamic and autocratic chancellor, Chief Justice Sir John Morris, who considered staff to be mere servants of the council; nor from the vice-chancellor, Torleiv Hytten. In later years Hytten wrote of the staff unrest with contempt: 'Most professors consider themselves to be prima donnas' was his opinion.[27] But otherwise students and staff were united in their desire for reform, with the student newspaper, *Togatus*, leading the charge. Following denunciation of the government in *Togatus* a series of anonymous letters in the *Mercury* further fanned the flames of dissent. Much of this activity was sponsored by the publicity committee of the staff association set up in mid-October. Prime movers in the group were academics Malcolm McCrae, George Wilson, Gerald Firth and John Polya, along with administrators Tony Kearney and Geoff Harrison. Orr too was a member of this committee, although a relatively silent one until, out of the blue, he proposed a full frontal attack in the form of an open letter to the premier calling for a royal commission into conditions at the university.

Even to his most radical colleagues Orr looked like a loose cannon and his immoderate language was too inflammatory. He was a latecomer to the agitation for change and was prepared to contribute little other than rhetoric. Ken Dallas noted that Orr 'liked to see himself as a rebel ("One of my ancestors was killed at Vinegar Hill") of the Mr Proddy kind', but Dallas, and others, felt he was 'just a bloody nuisance'.[28] Dallas was a Marxist economist with a reputation as a 'fellow traveller' who was utterly scornful of Orr's anti-communist posturing. He was dead against Orr's idea. Another opposing the move was fellow member of the publicity committee, historian WA Townsley, who had his doubts about Orr's motives having already experienced the less gallant side of Orr, who had threatened him 'that he was a Professor and I was not, and I should be careful of my tactics if I wanted to get anywhere.' Following his refusal to support Orr, Townsley found that Orr had his house under surveillance, sitting outside it in his car every afternoon. Anonymous and abusive phone calls also followed.[29] Together Dallas and Townsley sponsored a staff association motion to censure the professor of philosophy.

Nevertheless, after considerable moderation of the content, Orr persuaded thirty-seven colleagues to co-sign the letter published in the *Mercury* on 29 October. Among those who refused to sign the letter was Milanov, whose terror of retribution made him shy away from the merest hint of conflict. Knowing Orr's personal vulnerability he begged his professor not to go ahead with the flamboyant gesture. Another colleague who signed, with severe reservations, was Professor Warren Carey, who had been trying to negotiate with the chancellor on improved working conditions and new buildings. He disliked the emotionalism of Orr's missive but was smarting under the contempt of council members. He was well aware that the letter would be interpreted by the chancellor, who was his close friend, as an attack on his person and that his response would very likely ignite open warfare. So it did.

When Orr's inflammatory letter charging the university administration with 'apathy, neglect and maladministration' was published, the effect was electric. In the furore, the Opposition, seizing on the weakness of a minority government, forced a royal commission into the university administration; it opened at Parliament House in February 1955. It was a savage adversarial combat, with the counsel for the university, Senator Reg Wright, flaying the academic staff unmercifully. The bruising process permanently damaged the health of Professor Taylor, who had initially sought a parliamentary inquiry from the government. Others who led the staff case, such as Professor Carey and Professor Barber, also took a battering. In vain colleagues sought to stop Orr from appearing, fearing that his unpredictable and aberrant behaviour might further harm their cause. Even those who had signed his letter had concerns about him. John Polya, perhaps the most radical of the staff association, was driven to comment that Orr 'had forced us to abandon a reasoned, moderate, yet striking public letter so that his banshee wails might capture the limelight'.[30]

As professor of philosophy Orr did make a submission to the commission, making grandiose claims for philosophy's role in countering the indoctrination of communism. In the face of this constant threat to 'eliminate our democratic way of life, our freedom of choice and our liberty', he suggested that it would be unwise to leave the future leaders of the community 'without a complete and thoroughgoing philosophical training'.[31] With what I now realise is a cruel irony, Orr concluded by asserting that the University of Tasmania could become the St Andrews of the antipodes. After such lofty considerations, Orr was quite unprepared for a confrontation with Reg Wright, who made the accusation that Orr's lectures had plagiarised those of Professor Boyce Gibson. Notes taken by a student in Orr's lectures coincided remarkably with roneoed notes from Melbourne University and two students had complained of this to the vice-chancellor.

Sent into a tailspin by this suggestion, Orr went to the house of a mature-age student, the gifted and mercurial artist Edwin Tanner, excitedly demanding a copy of his notes since, Tanner recalls, Orr believed his notes would be different. 'Of course they would be different,' Tanner wrote. 'My notes were full of the sketches of girls' necks ... and I had also written some things about Orr, for he was a promising character for a novel.' However, it was not for these reasons that Tanner demurred. He believed Orr had used Boyce Gibson's notes, because he had sat beside a student with a copy and read as Orr repeated the material verbatim. Not that he was fussed by that. 'I didn't give a damn whose notes he used provided he used something that made sense. The trouble was the notes ... were not used often enough.'[32]

Orr was wounded by the royal commission, but then so was

almost everyone. Despite a terrible thrashing from Reg Wright, the academic case stood up well and the three commissioners accepted their arguments and criticised the paternalistic intervention of Chancellor Morris; drew attention to the weak administration of Vice-Chancellor Hytten; and recommended the establishment of a new and more broadly based council. Hytten and Morris were profoundly dismayed and embittered by the finding. As it became apparent that a new council would not automatically be created, Orr and other vocal critics such as John Polya, Malcolm McCrae and George Wilson felt they had cause to look to their backs. Polya was convinced that following the royal commission the university had hired private detectives to keep surveillance on all four of these academics. Still later he was sure that attempts had been made to kill him.[33]

If Sydney Sparkes Orr was having difficulty keeping control of his world in 1954, by 1955 he had completely lost it. Students who had been tolerantly bemused, even entertained, by Orr's lectures began to find the content bore little relationship to a philosophy course. 'You never knew what was going to happen,' one student recalls; 'I thought he was going crackers.' As she describes it, Orr would come into lectures waving the hem of his academic gown and perch on the wide windowsill and chain-smoke, all the while launching into his current obsession—his new house, insurance companies, the university administration ... and free love. Most members of the class were mature-age students—either teachers or returned servicemen—and were not pleased to be entertained in this fashion. Several grumbled and spoke of making a formal complaint.[34] Edwin Tanner gives a similar account of Orr's performance: 'giggling and parading in his gown ... he talked about Christian love and brotherly love and free love ... he couldn't stick to the discipline of the Platonic arguments we were to study. Sometimes I thought he was not well.'[35]

Several ex-students remember that the talk about free love was frequent, and was accompanied by lewd sexual innuendo.

Suzanne Kemp confided in her diary early in 1955 that 'Professor Orr talks so much about sex, I believe it must mean a lot in his life.' In court, Edwin Tanner told how, during these discourses on love Orr singled out the girls for concentrated attention:

> I would hate to misjudge him, but there was always a feeling of discomfort and I did feel for some of these girls, and I felt sure that when he discussed these points they seemed to be very uncomfortable.

So blatant was Orr's interest in the girl students that one group of undergraduate men considered playing a prank by dressing up as a female and making an assignation to meet Orr on the Post Office steps. He rearranged one class which initially had no women students. *Where are the girls?* were his first words to the amusement of the class. Next week there were female participants.[36]

While Suzanne responded to her professor's attention, she found it disconcerting to begin with: 'Just the way he looked and the way he spoke [showed] he was more interested in me than he should have been.' In a superbly whimsical painting done in 1954 Tanner caught the mood of these philosophy classes. Titled *The Philosopher King*, the painting presents the lecturer in billowing gown as a leering bat hovering above the blackboard on which there are no notes but only a heart shot through with Cupid's arrow. Singled out from the group, on a chair beside the blackboard, is a girl, the object of the bat's leering attention.

Yet another theme which recurred increasingly in Orr's lectures throughout 1955 was martyrdom. 'I shall either be canonised or crucified,' one student remembers him stating,[37] while Edwin Tanner recalls how Orr 'got terribly excited about a catholic martyr Patrick Hamilton, burned and buried under the gates of St Andrews so that anyone who entered the place would be reminded of his martyrdom ... he went on about Hamilton and martyrdom and Socrates and hemlock ... I couldn't bear seeing a man beside himself as Orr was.'[38] Moreover, as Suzanne Kemp was to testify in court and her diary, Orr was given to drawing parallels between himself and Jesus, martyred on the cross.

Professor Orr's unorthodox approach did have its enthusiasts nonetheless. A small coterie of students had formed the Socratic Society, which met regularly with Orr at a Hobart pub. Suzanne Kemp was the secretary. For this group, Orr was a dynamic and vibrant force shaking out the authoritarian and old-fashioned fuddy-duddies who ran the university. One clever, mature-age student, Jan Locher, who had fought with the Czech partisans during the war, thoroughly enjoyed Orr's iconoclastic and freewheeling discourse during lectures, as did the young Phillip Lake, who felt Orr opened up new intellectual horizons. Both liked to go drinking with Orr after classes to continue the argument and banter. Students who wrote testimonials for him stressed his inspirational lecture style and his accessibility. Most emphasised his willingness to help with students' emotional and personal problems.[39]

Orr was under increasing stress after the royal commission and because he was building a new house in Sandy Bay. It was this house which particularly impressed Orr upon Edwin Tanner, who claimed that Orr plagued him endlessly for free help and advice with the design and building. 'I couldn't shake Orr off: he was like a maggot on a chop.'[40] In what Tanner estimated were thirty or forty uninvited visits to his home he and his wife were treated to tearful accounts of Orr's illegitimacy and the personal tragedy of his having found then lost 'the most beautiful thing in the world'. His children tell me that they learnt to recognise the sound of Orr's car and would warn their father to hide before Orr was able to seek him out. Even though he came to hugely resent these intrusions, and grew increasingly contemptuous of Orr, Tanner had reason to be wary in his dealings with him. Following one rebuff, he found that an essay marked A by Milanov had been reduced to a lower grade by the professor.

Edwin Tanner, brilliant though he may have been, had come to university with stars in his eyes, having worked his way up from a position as an unskilled fourteen-year-old labourer at Port Kembla to be a senior engineer at 'the Hydro' (Hydro-Electricity Commission). His real passion was painting and poetry and he had gone to university to study aesthetics. 'Dad was very naive in many ways,' his son Jan recalls. 'He thought he was entering a hallowed temple for learning where the academic staff were the source of all true knowledge.'[41] For Tanner, professors were to be approached with humility and awe, so to be exposed to Orr's erratic and intellectually sloppy modus operandi was most upsetting.

Tanner had a high opinion of Milanov, for all his heavy accent and anxious, reclusive style. In contrast to Orr, he found Milanov a rigorous and demanding teacher with an impressive intellectual range; an opinion echoed by a number of fellow philosophy students who went on to distinguished careers in later life. Not so Professor Orr. By early 1955 he had quite reversed his opinion of the émigré philosopher, who was no longer providing him with psychoanalytical sessions. Vivian Smith, who had an office adjoining Orr's, recalls hearing the professor berating his only member of staff. Orr demanded copies of Milanov's lecture notes and, when these were not given, insisted on tape-recording the lectures. Ex-students report that Orr was openly ridiculing Milanov while sitting in on his classes, making faces and looking bored. Another colleague, Ken Dallas, was aware of Orr's persecution of Milanov and made some inquiries of his own. A student confirmed to him that he had written Orr an account of Milanov's comments on Plato 'knowing (he says) it would provoke lively discussion. Orr came into the next tute and forced M to recant in front of the whole class.' Dallas' own conviction was that Orr wanted to get rid of Milanov 'because Orr was incompetent as a philosopher and his energies found outlets in these tortured steps to safeguard his own position'. It was only later that Dallas realised Orr had been concerned about his psychoanalytical sessions. Milanov had 'kept mum' about these extramural responsibilities.[42] In April the chairman of the professorial board, Professor Carey, tried to conciliate between the two, with only limited success; he feared that 'the argument had become deeply personal, not intellectual.'[43]

Despite Carey's best efforts, tensions remained. Orr sought critical response to Milanov's courses from the science faculty without consulting his lecturer. He also encouraged students from the Socratic Club to write letters complaining about Milanov's teaching. One of these was Suzanne Kemp, who wrote up her interview with Orr in his room one evening prior to a late-night drive. 'He wanted to talk about Dr Milanov. Really his situation is very bad ... At this time when P. Orr is in such an unenviable position, this—a mishap in his department—is the worst thing that could happen. I can't help him.' Suzanne, a serious and clever student, was inclined to think Milanov could be worth listening to.

Milanov claims that on 29 April Orr subjected him to an harangue lasting many hours during which he was accused of trying to blackmail Orr with the record of his psychoanalysis. There followed a hair-raising drive to Milanov's house to recover the records of Orr's dreams. Milanov described Orr as nearly hysterical and incoherent on the return trip, and he found himself dumped unceremoniously in the middle of the city. Having made his way to the university, he was again confronted by his professor, who insisted that he was nor to return after the weekend and that Orr would henceforth take his courses. Timid and traumatised though he may have been, this last was too much for Milanov. He was fifty, had given up his permanent job and had no superannuation. The following Monday he took a formal complaint to the vice-chancellor. It was a matter of principle. 'I think academic freedom is valid for lecturers also and not for professors only,' he said.[44]

Professor Hytten had no love for Sydney Orr. He was bitter and angry about Orr's flamboyant gesture which had contributed to the humiliations of the royal commission. He was aware, from Professor Carey and others, that Orr was dropping heavy hints, whilst displaying the distinctive profile, that he was the son of Edward VIII. He had heard persistent rumours about Orr being seen with a girl student and he had been told by the bishop of Orr's ménage in Melbourne. Sorely regretting the decision to appoint Orr, he now believed he had been landed with a dud. 'I was furious with the Melbourne people as his testimonials from them had described him as a perfect gentleman and it was obvious they knew the whole story.'[45] The way things looked to Hytten 'there was a lot of trouble around ... and a great deal of it could be traced to Professor Orr.'[46] He thought it was time to get these issues documented.

Hytten knew of Townsley's run-ins with Orr and had in 1954 asked him to make a complaint which Townsley had refused because he didn't want to undermine staff association solidarity. In August 1955 the vice-chancellor found Townsley was prepared to put his grievances on paper. In essence he complained that Orr had intimidated and harassed him and threatened to interfere with his academic advancement. That month Hytten also had an interview with Bishop Cranswick at Bishopcourt. The bishop was concerned about rumours of Orr's 'vicious liaison' with a young woman (not Suzanne Kemp). Whether there was any truth to this rumour, or whether it had been fed to the bishop in order that he disclose confidences about Orr, is a matter of much conjecture. The bishop himself had serious doubts about this some years later. At the time he was sufficiently angry to show the two professors A's letters to him with their candid and unflattering portrait of Orr. These letters showed, the bishop felt, 'that Sydney Orr exerts a fascination over young people'.[47] Cranswick followed his action by writing a letter to the newspaper suggesting the university would be well served if some staff (unnamed) were to leave.

One complaint for which Professor Hytten was unprepared, and one he did not welcome, arrived on his desk on 2 December

1955. It came from Edwin Tanner and concerned Professor Orr's requests for personal favours 'so near to the examinations that I experienced a feeling of personal obligation'. The most recent request, made just after his exams but before the results, was the last straw. Tanner claimed Orr had asked him, a painter of note, to paint a mural in his new home, giving clear hints that Tanner would receive the philosophy prize in return. Since Tanner had hopes of this prize he felt the message was that he could not expect success without the return of a favour. 'It seems unreasonable,' Tanner wrote, 'that an undergraduate, even a mature one, should feel that his academic success depends on his ability to satisfy the private requests of a professor.'[48]

News of the Tanner complaint hit the staff association executive like a body blow. Soon after, to his amazement, Tanner claims he was confronted in his private office by a wild-eyed secretary of the staff association, Malcolm McCrae, who pleaded with him to reconsider. As Tanner recalls, McCrae said to him 'we all know Orr is mad, but we have to protect the staff.'[49]

An even wilder confrontation took place outside Tanner's office when Professor Orr came to see him. 'He raved at me about ruining him and his family and said he was going to kill me. I walked off ... he was crying—crying in a public place. I weakened; I was overcome with compassion. I asked him to come into the park opposite to talk. I hated seeing a man like that.' In the park Orr resumed his diatribe and Tanner walked away. 'Orr grabbed my coat. I just kept going with Orr in tow—through the gate, up the stone steps ...' Having been dragged 'some thirty yards [he] dropped off my coat and started psychoanalysing me from afar.'[50]

At the university Orr attempted to deal with the Tanner affair by dismissing it as the aberration of a student 'notorious for getting bees in his bonnet'. He gave the vice-chancellor a formal reply to the Tanner complaints, denying he had made requests for favours and denying all but a few brief visits to the Tanner house. Most interestingly, he said that matters to do with his house had cropped up during one of Tanner's regular visits to him 'to discuss his personal and psychological and professional difficulties resulting from what he alleged to be inadequate recognition of his artistic talents'.[51] It did not take long for Tanner to find that stories were circulating of his having mental illness and 'cracking up'.[52]

Not everyone was so readily convinced that this was a crackpot student, as Orr was to discover on 15 December when he attended the staff Christmas party. 'There was a strained atmosphere of foreboding, with the men getting together into groups and talking guardedly,' he told an associate in England. The rumour was that a complaint against Orr was to go to council the following day. Orr tackled his old ally, Professor Carey, who told him: 'Look here, Sydney, if I were you I should take this seriously ... your professional career may end tomorrow.'[53]

After a tense day of discussions behind closed doors, the complaints against Orr were presented to the council. Chancellor Sir John Morris 'was not impressed'.[54] Furthermore, as he warned the other members, he was not about to give any impression that Orr was being victimised as a result of his outspoken stance. He was supported in this by the other legal expert on council, state solicitor-general Stanley Burbury, who was to succeed Morris as chief justice. But the professors on the council, staunch staff association members all, saw it differently. They felt the complaints had to be investigated since 'the allegations were very serious, involving Professor Orr's fitness to be a professor.' The council moved to set up a committee to investigate the matter in the New Year.

The gravity of the situation was not lost on the more active members of the staff association. Next day executive members Gerald Firth and Malcolm McCrae took Orr on a nightmarish drive to Burnie ('Never drive with a Platonist'), to get legal advice from Hamish Gow, recently resigned from the law faculty. Gow wanted to ensure that due process was observed and that Orr's rights were protected. Orr himself he found a problematic client. 'How ever could that man get to be a Professor of Philosophy?' he asked Firth in a bemused aside.[55]

In the meantime, sympathetic students were busy in Orr's defence. One student close to Orr, John Biggs, undertook to collect testimonials about Orr's teaching and character. Suzanne Kemp wrote one of these, dated 19 December 1955. On the same day the vice-chancellor received a letter from Gow demanding the particulars of the complaints and the procedures to be followed. These he did not get, causing him to reply 'I have heard of the Divine right of Kings but never of the Divine right of Vice-Chancellors.'[56]

Over the holidays Orr became aware that rumours about his personal life were growing apace—not only talk of his love life in Melbourne, but also talk about his relationships with girl students in Hobart, one girl student in particular. In February, student supporters, this time organised by SRC president Malcolm Hills, were again asked to make statements of support; specifically, female students were asked to declare that their relationships with the professor were quite proper. Once again Suzanne Kemp, against her father's wishes, wrote a testimonial. From the staff there was no action.

The committee appointed to investigate the allegations against Orr was to meet on 24 February 1956. It was with amazement, then, that the professorial members of the committee—Carey, Elliott and Pitman—read in the *Mercury* of 16 February that £10 000 writs for libel had been issued against them, as well as Townsley, recently appointed as professor of political science, who was a complainant. Clearly the writs were meant as intimidation to prevent the committee from proceeding. It was a move that did nothing to enhance Orr's standing in the academic community. In any case, the committee did not meet. Its business was overtaken by the council meeting of 2 March and the dramatic appearance of Reginald Kemp, complaining that his daughter had been seduced.

At this last bombshell the already frantic members of the

staff association were devastated. Geoff Harrison, the university accountant who had had occasion to rebuke Orr about Suzanne Kemp months earlier, met some of his fellow members at the university gates saying: 'Syd Orr has pooed in our nest.'[57]

CHAPTER FOUR

I hold it to be misconduct for a professor to seduce his student

Bill Oats remembers the university council meeting of 2 March with great clarity. Newly appointed, he found that the meetings, held in a gloomy, cavernous room in the basement of the original stone building, were not pleasant occasions. This one was especially awful. The door flew open and Reg Kemp stormed in, saying: 'Professor Orr has seduced my daughter. I want you to dismiss him.'[58] The overwhelming mood of the meeting was outrage. Another serious complaint against Orr hard on the heels of the Tanner complaint. What was the fellow going to do next? When the dramatic tension of Kemp's appearance had subsided, Professor Hytten produced Orr's resignation, which he had received that morning from Orr's solicitor. The council was faced with the choice of pursuing the allegations against Orr or accepting his immediate resignation with six months pay in lieu of notice. Hytten took the view that the council should accept the resignation 'not because I did not think he deserved dismissal, but because I dimly saw the trouble ahead' if Orr were sacked.[59]

Now, the vice-chancellor need not have taken Orr's resignation to council, if he had wanted to avoid trouble. He could have accepted it that morning, as the accountant Geoff Harrison practically begged him to do, and merely informed council of his executive decision. Then the Kemp issue need not have become public, and the university would be spared the otherwise inevitable scandal, Harrison argued. Well he might have argued. He and Malcolm McCrae had been up most of the night before trying to persuade Orr to write the resignation.[60] Orr's legal advisor, Hamish Gow, had first suggested this course of action when he realised how desperate was Orr's position. At a meeting with Hytten two days earlier he had flagged the possibility of resignation, and the vice-chancellor had given him to understand he would welcome it. The hard work was to persuade a very reluctant Orr.

He finally agreed early on the morning of the council meeting because he could see no support for his case among his colleagues. Even John Polya had turned against him, believing that 'his indiscretions endangered most of the gains made by the progressive minority of the staff'.[61] Years later Orr was to claim that the resignation was a mistake and that he had written it without prejudice in order to protect his family from the public exposure of his previous relationship with A. He insisted it was in no way an admission of guilt in relation to the Kemp charge. That was not Geoff Harrison's view. He was furious that Orr had dragged the university into a terrible mess. 'I could have killed the little b myself.' But he also understood that powerful forces in the community had 'pointed the bone' at Sydney Orr from the moment of his open letter to the premier. He knew that if the Kemp allegations got to the council Orr would be 'a goner' and that the university too would be hurt in the fallout.[62]

Hytten may have been formally correct in taking the resignation to council, but his motive for doing so is suspect given that he allowed an overwrought Reg Kemp to address the council before introducing the resignation. Harrison was right that the council was in no mood to accept the resignation, but not necessarily because of a desire to 'get Orr'. Bill Oats, a Quaker and supporter of unpopular political causes, was in no way part of the Hobart establishment, yet he agreed with the rest of the council that the allegations against Orr must be tested to see whether Orr could be said to have breached the high standard of behaviour expected of academics. This was a position from which he never resiled, despite some vigorous latter-day lobbying from those who felt Orr had suffered an injustice.

Mr Kirby from Electrolytic Zinc, reflected the general mood of the meeting when, moving to reject the resignation, he argued fervently that the university had a moral responsibility to not simply move a wayward professor on to some other unsuspecting campus. Support was unanimous. If some members believed that Orr should not be granted six months salary because it would give him the economic wherewithal to pursue the five writs he currently had against fellow professors and Mr Kemp, this was not the overwhelming sentiment. Sir John Morris, who had been so cautious previously, agreed that the resignation should not be accepted, because of his belief in the importance of teacher–student relationships.

In Morris' opinion 'the council moved on this one with great circumspection ... meticulous to observe the principles of natural justice.'[63] A sub-committee including legal experts HS Baker and Stanley Burbury was established to inquire into the Kemp charge, to which were added a professorial representative Professor Pitman, and the vice-chancellor. The chairman of the staff association, Professor Barber, was also co-opted. The vice-chancellor was directed to inquire into the Townsley, Milanov and Tanner allegations, assisted by professors Carey, Elliot, Pitman and Barber. Professor Orr was informed in writing the same day of the Kemp allegations and directed to meet the committee to answer them on Friday 9 March 1956. He was also suspended from duty and instructed not to attend the university or conduct academic business with students.

Hamish Gow had withdrawn from the case and Orr had since sought the advice of Hobart MHA Bill Hodgman, a lawyer, who was that Friday in Melbourne, briefing a senior counsel on Orr's behalf. His request to represent Orr at the inquiry was denied on the grounds that this was in no sense a formal or legal inquiry, but an investigation, to be conducted in the same way any employer would investigate any serious charge against an employee.

When Orr faced the committee on 9 March he followed Hodgman's advice and made only a categoric denial, making it clear he was not prepared to answer the charges, to make a public statement or to call witnesses in his support. He was convinced that the dice was loaded against him and that he was facing a star chamber. Recalling his feelings that day, he wrote 'for the first time in my life I realized something of what it must be like to fall foul of a totalitarian regime.'[64] In response to his concern about his legal rights the committee adjourned over the weekend to allow Orr to consult his lawyer. On the Monday, Hodgman himself made an appearance, telling the committee he believed they had gone beyond the bounds of a master-servant relationship, and that the issues would have to be dealt with in court. Orr would reserve his defence until then. The only deliberation the committee should concern itself with was whether to summarily dismiss the professor or whether to accept his resignation with six months salary, he said.

Not prepared to accept Hodgman's interpretation, the committee proceeded to hear evidence in Orr's presence. Reg Kemp outlined his discovery of Suzanne's affair with Orr and how he had gone to the professor's house and assaulted him. During this evidence Orr broke his own rule to ask several questions on Suzanne's psychological state. 'Did I not say to you,' he asked Kemp 'that your daughter had come to me for help and that I told her at one stage after I saw how disturbed she was that she should see a psychiatrist ...?' Kemp did not agree. Nor did he agree that Orr had told him that it was 'a perfectly normal phenomenon' for someone to develop a fixation on the person from whom they had been getting psychological help.

Suzanne also gave evidence about her developing relationship with Orr over a period of ten months. With some embarrassment and the help of a loose-leaf diary (mostly written in German), she detailed sexual encounters in various locations between June and December. She gave rough translations of several incriminating entries, which she elaborated under close questioning from Solicitor-General Burbury. Orr was drawn to question her on one point. Why, he wanted to know, had she written a letter saying her relationship with him was quite proper? 'Because I believed in you and believed that you thought you were doing right,' she replied. 'I thought you were doing right and I wanted to defend you.' He also asked if she had come to him for psychological help. 'I just came to discuss things,' she said. 'Maybe after I had been talking to you for a long time I had decided that maybe I was a bit queer, but when I came in the beginning I did not have that idea.'

Orr repeatedly refused to answer any questions relating to Suzanne, even such questions as those his lawyer had permitted, leaving the frustrated staff association representative, Professor Barber, to despair that 'I have fought for three months for this opportunity [to answer charges] to be granted to Professor Orr' and now Orr seemed intent on throwing his chance away. It was he who arranged for three students to address the committee about Suzanne. These were Jan Locher and Phil Lake, members of the Socratic Society who had previously written to complain of Dr Milanov, and a young woman who was not a philosophy student. They said that Suzanne had had a crush on the professor and appeared to them to be somewhat fanciful in her response to men: twice before she had suggested that some other man had tried to seduce her in a car en route to a parry.

The committee chairman and the vice-chancellor made a last desperate attempt to induce Orr to defend himself, pointing out that the committee would make a conclusive recommendation. 'I can't help that' was Orr's reply. The committee found the allegations to be true and recommended dismissal. It remained for the internal investigations to be held the following morning. This time Orr protested that he had been denied a full written statement of allegations against him, and promptly withdrew. In his absence the five professors agreed that 'Professor Orr has not proved capable of conducting his department ... he is quite unfitted to be a professor in this university.' Summary dismissal followed on Friday 16 March 1956.

A writ for wrongful dismissal was served on the university on Monday 19 March. Writing to an old friend about this turn of events, the chief justice observed: 'I doubt that he will ever proceed with his action and probably he hopes the issue of a writ will stifle discussion and prevent wide currency of the reasons of his dismissal. Perhaps he will even allege victimization in consequence of the exercise of his right of free speech'.[65] Sir John Morris did not live long enough to observe that he was wrong in his first assumption, but absolutely correct with his second.

Within the staff there was some small sympathy for Orr, who had been abruptly rendered penniless and unemployed. He had, after all, come up with a resignation. In a last-minute attempt at negotiation, Orr's barrister, Esler Barber, QC, proposed to the university that Orr would not pursue the litigation if the Council agreed to six months pay in lieu of notice. The council refused—a very costly failure of judgement, as it transpired. Orr's court case looked set to be rougher and dirtier than the royal commission, Gerald Firth informed the absent Ken Dallas, echoing the widely held feeling that 'it will be as much the fault of the people who preferred to ignore the resignation as of wretched Orr himself.' Still, Firth admitted, 'much as I deplore the manner of his going, the atmosphere is much clearer without him.' The university was bracing itself for this 'last ordeal', Firth reported in June, and 'already the air is clearer and the clouds are lifting'.[66]

When they approached the Supreme Court, Orr's lawyers, Hodgman and Barber, had hoped to confine the case to the particulars of Orr's contract, which specified only that he was employed till the age of sixty-five and so could not be dismissed for any other reason. Orr had other ideas and was determined to contest all the items of misconduct alleged, providing a packed court and a bevy of eager reporters from mainland newspapers with a feast of salacious detail. Most legal commentators regarded this tactic as misguided, if not disastrous. Orr should never have been allowed into the witness box. His counsel were of that opinion also, but failed to prevail against Orr's overweening egotism. As Ken Dallas saw it, Orr was determined to use the court as a soapbox. 'Name me a lawyer in Australia who could have kept Orr out of the witness box,' Dallas challenged a legal friend; 'his confidence in his self righteousness was such that he believed the world (his world?) would be convinced of it once he had spoken.' Rejecting any parallel with Dreyfus, Dallas saw that Oscar Wilde was the obvious model for Orr: 'the same arrogance, rushing into law and exposing himself to criminal prosecution, discrediting and ruin'.[67]

After eighteen days of evidence, during which Orr was recalled several times, Justice Green concluded that 'Miss Kemp is speaking the truth, while the plaintiff is not.' His Honour found the university was justified in dismissing Orr on the ground of his misconduct with Suzanne Kemp, saying:

> He used his position as her professor to seduce her. It was as her professor he secured her confidence and asked her to visit him ... It was from his position of authority as a professor that he discussed with her the idea of a relationship outside marriage and feeling as being the basis for living ... Such conduct amounts to a complete repudiation of the duty which a professor owes to his university ... it seems to me to be essential, if the integrity of the university is to be preserved, that a professor should maintain a detached and dispassionate attitude toward his students ... it was put to me in the course of argument that this case is of great importance to the academic world, because involved in it is some question as to the security of the position of professors and lecturers everywhere. I must confess I do not quite appreciate how this is put. So far as I am

> concerned I am holding that a university professor is just as liable to be dismissed for misconduct as any other servant ... I hold it to be misconduct for a professor to seduce his student.

Justice Green then detailed his reasons for believing Suzanne's evidence over Orr's. She kept a diary admitted in evidence, and conceded by Orr's counsel, which was contemporaneous with the events described and which details information she could scarcely have got from anyone other than Orr. If her accounts of her meetings with Orr were merely fantasy, Green decided, 'it is incredible that she should have the cleverness to have attempted to give reality to the fantasy by writing such matters into it even if she knew them.' She was also able to produce gifts from Orr, including a pair of earrings. The jeweller had positively identified Orr as the man who bought those earrings. Another witness was called who, Suzanne claimed, had pulled Orr's car from a ditch when they had become stuck late one night at an isolated spot on Bellerive beach. Orr gave a quite different account of this event which the judge did not believe. 'I am quite unable to understand, in any case,' he concluded 'how the plaintiff's visit to Bellerive fitted into his story that his relationship between himself and Miss Kemp was a mere relationship of professor and student.' There was the letter from Orford, which he found most telling: 'One would have thought that on the receipt of such a letter from an ordinary student who meant nothing to him he would have taken immediate steps to check any ideas and put a stop to them ... but the plaintiff did none of these things.' Finally, Justice Green had to ask what possible motive did Suzanne have for inventing her story? He could find none.

As for the allegations concerning Milanov, Townsley and Tanner, these did not justify summary dismissal. In some cases, such as his behaviour with Edwin Tanner, Green believed Orr was 'thoughtless and completely misjudged', but his actions did not amount to misconduct. 'It may well be that they show, taken together, that the plaintiff was an unsatisfactory Professor,' was Green's ultimate conclusion.

An appeal against Green's judgement was lodged with the High Court in May 1957, claiming that he was wrong in law in his interpretation of the contract; in his interpretation of misconduct; in his use of evidence to corroborate Suzanne's oral testimony; in his having admitted certain evidence; and in making a finding inconsistent with and contrary to the evidence. The appeal was led by an outstanding QC from Melbourne, Ashkenasy, who argued the case before justices Taylor, Williams and Dixon. To his glee, Reg Wright, appearing for the university, was not even required to put a case.

The High Court judges found there were no grounds to justify their intervention, noting that in law Suzanne Kemp's evidence did not need to be corroborated and that Green had considered the letter and diary merely as factors on which he placed some reliance. Moreover, the material introduced to the prejudice of Orr was properly admitted and properly used. 'There is not the slightest reason why his honour should have doubted Miss Kemp's evidence on the vital matters which arose for his decision. On the contrary there is much to support it and much to destroy that given by the appellant.' And they went further: 'We have not the slightest doubt that ... the university was entitled to dismiss him. We can only express our surprise that the contrary should be maintained.' Orr was shattered. 'I am bankrupt. I am ruined,' he told waiting reporters.[68]

Can it be fairly said, as it has so often been said in the years that followed Orr's dismissal, that the university had acted improperly in dealing with Orr? The Federal Council of the University Staff Associations (FCUSA) belatedly came to believe it had, when they investigated the dismissal of Orr over three years later, reporting that 'the University of Tasmania in the procedures which led to Professor Orr's dismissal manifestly failed to accord him natural justice.' It claimed that too many people on the inquiry were likely to be biased against Orr; that Orr was denied legal counsel and forced to conduct his defence alone and unaided; and that Orr did not have enough precise detail of the charges against him to organise a refutation. The whole procedure was unfair and 'forced Orr into the position of plaintiff in an action' by refusing to accept his tendered resignation.[69] It was this conclusion that the university had denied natural justice to Orr which was the basis for a crippling censure and a black ban on the chair of philosophy imposed on the university between 1958 and 1966. (By no means all mainland academics saw the issue that way. From Sydney University the professor of mathematics wrote to the newspapers to suggest that 'if natural justice is primitive justice, then someone might well have been pushed over a cliff before he set foot in Tasmania.'[70])

As Hal Wootten pointed out in his article in *Quadrant* in 1957, because the council lacked any established procedures for dealing with matters of academic misconduct, it failed to do a number of things to ensure natural justice for Orr. Hytten was too partisan to be included on the committee, and Orr should have had the benefit of counsel or someone of his own choosing from the staff association to assist him. He should have been given the full particulars of the allegations against him. Perhaps, too, following the inquiry Orr should have been given six months pay in lieu of notice, rather than be abruptly made jobless and penniless. Had the council been prepared to act with that degree of magnanimity, it is possible that the Orr case would not have become any more than an academic footnote. However the university saw itself under no obligation, moral or legal, to be so meticulous or magnanimous. The council was not obliged to hold an inquiry at all and did so, as John Morris insisted, to give Orr the essence of justice—the right to confront his accusers, question them and call witnesses in his defence.

That he chose not to exercise that right may be understandable, given his belief that he was being set up, but he denied himself due process. It was Orr, after all, who insisted that the university had no jurisdiction to investigate the charges and that they would have to be resolved in the courts.

Conceding that the inquiry fell short of ideal standards of natural justice, what is essential, as Hal Wootten makes clear, is that 'none of these shortcomings affected the ultimate position of Orr, who despite the Committee's findings went to the court on the basis he was presumed innocent until affirmatively proved guilty.' Nor do any of these shortcomings 'supply any reason for doubting the correctness of the Committee's conclusions'. Some of the men on the university council did not like Orr, some responded emotionally as outraged parents, some, I have reason to believe, were prepared to be vindictive, but I cannot overlook the fact that they were faced with utterly plausible allegations of gross misconduct that Orr did nothing to refute. I just can't see how the outcome could have been otherwise, and I agree with Donald Horne, who said, 'perhaps academics who lend themselves to a deliberate undermining of a whole university are a greater menace to academic life than a university that committed errors in procedure in dismissing a philandering professor.'[71]

Mind you, I am not at all convinced that questions of 'natural justice' were those fuelling academic protest at the Orr decision. The more emotional issue, at least for those most vigorous in support of Orr, was the issue of the master-servant relationship. The council's position, upheld by the courts, was that it had the right to investigate allegations and dismiss on the ground of misconduct of a professional character, just as any employer has that right. Academic freedom is not *supra legen*—it gives no claim to superiority above the law. In this reading of the law of contracts, never disputed by the courts, all contracts between a university and its academic staff are contracts for service and can be terminated. The relationship is one of master to servant. Not so, insisted ex-professor Orr. The proper discharge of duties for an academic can only be decided by his academic peers within the community of scholars. The committee set up by council represented 'serious lay administrative interference with academic control' he claimed.[72] His mentor, Emeritus Professor Morris Miller, elaborated Orr's argument, insisting that an academic was in no way a servant but 'the master of his own domain of knowledge ... a free agent within the realm of learning ... in unfettered devotion to truth and in accordance with the standards determined by scholars through the ages.'[73] It stood to reason then that considerations of impropriety in that august realm should only be determined by scholars. In Sydney, Professor Alan Stout, alerted to the case by Morris Miller, was keen to emphasise that universities were societies, or associations, of scholars. He was 'deeply concerned by the apparent failure of the University of Tasmania to recognize the special nature and way of life that characterizes a university as a community of scholars'.[74] In Melbourne, Professor 'Panzee' Wright took up the cudgels against the very idea that a professor was 'a common servant' and not 'a member of a traditional community of scholars exercising its own proper right to accept or reject members'.[75]

Academic lawyers were unimpressed with this quaint interpretation, which, if it was relevant at all, applied only to Oxford and Cambridge with their unique institutions reaching back into medieval practice. When he was asked for legal opinion, Geoffrey Sawyer remarked: 'I have never been able to work up much excitement about the question of master and servant which so many academics seem to resent ... [I find] more than a touch of snobbery in the excitement'. In a mild reprimand, Sawyer reminded the staff associations that it was 'very bad propaganda for academics to kick up a song and dance about being called servants.'[76] As he quite rightly presumed, the general community did not care for the suggestion that academics were superior to the legal obligations which govern contracts of employment.

But kick up a song and dance they did, in staff associations across the country and in professional organisations in the United Kingdom. It was not a concern appreciated by the academics for whom the issue was most pertinent. As Roy Chappell, one of Orr's few sympathetic ex-colleagues, explained to prominent defender of intellectual freedom, George Polyani in Britain, '[Orr] is looked upon as man unworthy of support. Many of his colleagues hate and despise him, considering that he has done a great deal of harm to the university and deserves all his trouble'. Chappell himself believed Orr should have been allowed to resign but felt he was 'undoubtedly a fool and not a desirable person to have as a professor of anything—let alone philosophy'. In his opinion all the staff 'would be glad when the Orr case is over and he departs this island for good.' Provocatively he added: 'Would you like him in Manchester?'[77] What others in the Tasmanian community of scholars had to say was a good deal more virulent.

There is no doubt whatever that had an alternative procedure been adopted to deal with the allegations of misconduct, contained entirely within the academic preserve of the community of scholars, the outcome would have been substantially the same: Orr would have lost his job as professor of philosophy. The president of the staff association made this clear to Orr in 1957 in response to his request for a new inquiry: 'The Staff Association feels that different and preferable procedures, had they been adopted in the first place, or were they to be adopted at another enquiry now, would not, then or now, produce a different decision as to the facts. It does not seem to us that the procedures followed by the university, however faulty, did in fact lead to a miscarriage of justice in your case.'[78]

Of course it was easy to deride the academics in Hobart as being craven, self-interested and gutless, as they were often accused of being. In his *Prospect* articles Bill Ginnane was in especially good form, describing the Hobart campus as a place devoid of the moral conditions of a genuine university. Those who taught in this debased environment could not be said to represent a community of scholars since 'there is no community there concerned with, let alone dedicated to, truth. There is only the remnant of such a community.' In his opinion, this remnant had been systematically corrupted with academics 'ensnared in a web of fear and malice'. Bill Ginnane, who was in England until 1960, had not been to Tasmania, nor had most of his compatriots who spoke of their colleagues with such open contempt.

They perceived no moral dilemma in putting bans on the institution, placing academics in Hobart beyond the pale of the high-minded collegiate ideal, especially as they had no interest in seeking appointment to such a retarded backwater. In despair at the prospect of a ban, John McManners, the new professor of history, begged fellow academics to consider what they were doing to him and his colleagues. 'I cannot accept any lack of courage among the staff here. I was not here in the Royal Commission battle, but if you want resistance to authority did the University of Tasmania staff put up a fight then or not? The fact that we are not fighting in the Orr case in the same way ought surely to give you pause ... Why don't you—why didn't you—send a deputation here to us meet us all and see for yourself ... You are absolutely right in demanding courage from us. What are we entitled to expect from you?'[79]

No matter how some people attempted to dress it up, the concern with the master-servant relationship was a trade-union issue, to do with the protection of academic tenure and the terms and conditions of academic appointments, as FCUSA understood full well. Legal advice to individual staff associations and FCUSA was unambiguous that in law the contract between academic and staff was a contract for service, regardless of tenure, and all such contracts could be terminated summarily for grave misconduct. The real consideration, therefore, was how to ensure that tenure could not be easily broken and that rigorous processes be in place to determine the question of misconduct.

Whatever individuals may have thought, and said, the Orr case became a convenient stalking horse for a fledgling trade union wanting to flex some muscle at a time when universities in Australia were rapidly expanding. It was convenient, given that the University of Tasmania was small and located in a distant, parochial city that was derided as backward, authoritarian and bizarre, that it should become the focus for a campaign about terms and conditions of employment some four years after the dismissal of Professor Orr. For FCUSA the bottom line for the lifting of the censure which hung over the university was not reinstatement of Orr but the adoption of an acceptable tenure statute.

As for the specific allegations of impropriety against Orr, it was Orr himself who insisted that these could only be properly dealt with in the courts. But when the courts delivered a verdict which was not in his favour, they too came under attack from Orr and his latter-day academic supporters. The FCUSA report said he was convicted on evidence 'that would not hang a dog', which is probably true, if utterly misleading. Orr was not on trial, charged with a criminal offence. *Orr vs University of Tasmania* was a civil action and as such required a different standard of proof—that the case is proved on the balance of probabilities; not beyond all reasonable doubt. The case was a breach of contract; not a criminal trial for seduction.

It was further asserted that since Orr was necessarily the appellant rather than the accused he was forced to prove his innocence: 'nobody had to prove me guilty beyond reasonable doubt,' Orr complained, 'but I had to prove my innocence beyond reasonable doubt.'[80] This claim, as John Kerr and Hal Wootten pointed out in their examination of the legal issues, was nonsense. The university carried the legal burden of justifying Orr's dismissal and satisfying the judge that the allegations against him were true. The only verdict on Orr that his academic champions ever did accept was that of the inquiry of the Scots Kirk Session, the court of the Presbyterian Church of Tasmania, held in 1958. How fitting that those who claimed membership of the community of scholars would privilege an ecclesiastical court over the civil court and the High Court of Australia.

It seemed to those in Hobart who had stuck by Orr that the High Court judgement was the end of the road, and that he should take his family away and try to get another job elsewhere. That was not easy, as he had no money and substantial debts. Costs had been awarded against him in both court cases, he had two mortgages and there were two caveats on his large new house. The High Court appeal had been financed with a substantial loan from a solicitor and small donations from mainland staff associations. His family was dependent on personal donations from well-wishers. To sympathetic onlookers it seemed hopeless for him to stay, and for his family's sake they urged him to cut his losses and go. Roy Chappell argued on council that Orr should get some assistance to help him to rehabilitate himself and 'become a useful citizen in another field far removed from Hobart'. He was appalled at the callous reaction. No one would even second his motion.

Chappell's notes from the period record his profound concern for Orr's 'innocent family', forced to endure poverty and ignominy while Orr 'vainly hopes for a return to academic life'. In November 1957 Chappell gave Orr a lift and was shocked at his state: 'he was shaking with emotional disturbance, smoking furiously and he could speak only with difficulty. He told me he was finished, he was breaking up—he couldn't get work—his last hope of a retrial had gone ...' Chappell told him to pull himself together and to stop trying to sift and resist the evidence and get a job.[81]

Those who knew Orr well knew this advice would not be heeded. Two years earlier another supportive colleague,

George Wilson, had predicted that 'he will fight this till the day he dies.'[82] Others recognised that Orr had cast himself in the role of martyr and that this was to be his new career.[83] 'What would you do in my case?' Orr asked Chappell. 'Wouldn't you fight on if you knew you were innocent?' It was a question for which Chappell had no answer. 'I came away convinced that if Orr were confirmed in this mood, the tragedy would become even greater.'

CHAPTER FIVE

He has always been interested in his students

One of the disconcerting things about contemporary history of this kind is that the scars are still visible, the pain still palpable. Participants in the drama have not conveniently faded into vague memory. I am quite likely to bump into the woman who was once Suzanne Kemp in the supermarket, or encounter any of Sydney Orr's children at a party. How might I defend the unwelcome intrusion of a traumatic past into their present lives? Is my conscientious detective work any different from the salacious voyeurism of those newspaper reporters who filled the Hobart courthouse in 1956 to record every detail of intimate testimony?

To use a legalistic defence, I insist the public has a right to know, some thirty-five years down the track, what the issues in this business really were, once the layers of amnesia and deliberate distortion have been peeled away. If I were being really honest I'd have to add that I found a compelling story underneath the mythology, and I can't resist the storyteller's urge to reconstruct it; but that does not render me insensible to the moral dilemma. People will be hurt; I know that. When strangers ring me, usually anonymously and late at night, to tell me to leave well enough alone, I feel terrible. Yes, people will be hurt, but other people have already been hurt; profound, lasting damage has been done, sometimes to those who were no more than bystanders. And what of the person who said to me: 'Thank God someone is going to write about this, I have had to live with lies about me for thirty-five years and I want to be vindicated before I die'? Or Edwin Tanner, dead now for over ten years, who wrote out his 'hell and grief' in a sixty-eight-page document he left among his papers, unknown to his family? I knew as soon as I read it that his voice needed to be heard. There are others, mute but damaged. I want to say something on their behalf. So I tell my late-night callers: 'This is history; these events are on the public record.' Is that a fair thing? I'm not entirely sure. But I am up to my armpits in it now and couldn't give it away even if I wanted to.

I am telling you all of this because of yet another phone call last night and also because I know how shocked I was to encounter the newspaper reports, neatly clipped and pasted into archive ledgers. It was not that the material was new, I had read it all and more. What shocked me was the sense of a nation of eyes devouring intimate details so foolish, so tacky, so inevitably sordid. Is it possible for me to offer up that same fare without the titillation? But I can't take the sex out of the story: the sex is what the story is all about.

Like most eighteen-year-old girls, Suzanne Kemp was very interested in the opposite sex. The boys she met at parties or during rehearsals for the University Revue were scrutinised, in private, for signs that they might be the one she could love. She was, as the song goes, falling in love with love, but having difficulty finding an object of love and an outlet for her sexual turbulence. Not that the boys were aware of the incipient passion beneath Suzanne's cool exterior. She seemed very shy and aloof, to them, more interested in ideas and music than flirting; an intellectual ill-at-ease with adolescent horseplay. Her nickname among the lads was 'Kelvinator Kemp'. Jan Locher, something of a Lothario, with whom she was linked in later gossip, felt instinctively that she just wasn't the sexual kind. Too cold, too uptight, in his considered judgement. Neither he nor any of her male peer group to whom I spoke remembers scoring more than a timid kiss.

Her teachers, male and female, interested Suzanne more than the callow youths of her acquaintance and her diary admits to a crush on her German teacher (a woman) and her French tutor (a man) of which they were totally oblivious. They were aware of her intoxication with intellectual matters and how she felt a whole new world had opened up to her in contrast to the narrow bourgeois world of her parents. She devoured works by the French existentialists—Camus, Sartre and de Beauvoir. The idea that thinking was a valid activity was totally new to her and she revelled in it. Any intellectual input aroused her. In her diary she goes overboard for the ancient, and some would say dull, Sir John Shepherd, a visiting academic who gave a lecture on *Antigone*. In retrospect it is easy to see that she was ripe for the erotic spiritual combination that was fashionable in some intellectual circles. At the time she seemed like a sensible, healthy and hard-working student—all rosy cheeks and jolly hockey sticks.

The professor of philosophy, on the other hand, did notice something special about the starry-eyed young student. In her first year at university, in 1954, she had felt he had been lecturing to her, singling her out with his piercing eyes. When lectures began again in 1955 she felt drawn even more strongly to him and this worried her. So in April 1955 she begins to confide her feelings to her diary. 'I find my feelings for P Orr very childish ... very immature useless idiotic ... I will try and control my passions. But when one feels something one isn't inclined to pacify the feeling. Rather one encourages oneself to swim with the feeling. Not in the open, but in bed for example—or in one's heart ...'

She continued to notice his attention in classes and accepted a few lifts with him, along with other girls. And he 'showed some reaction to me after drinking quite a bit of whisky'. In April she had heard gossip about Orr having got a girl into trouble in Melbourne, 'and she was not the first.' This was tantalising: 'I can believe that and I feel a peculiar excitement. I don't admire him much. Is he honourable? If I can expect anything from him then No ... It makes life a bit more interesting if one has an object of feeling but if it goes any further what then?... It seems so ridiculous that a professor, married—should interest himself in a student. Still it does seem possible.' Alone with her feelings, Suzanne spent most of Sunday pondering this: 'One can argue that [it is wrong] only in relation to accepted moral behaviour, that if it is the natural expression of personality, if it is genuine feeling, then it is quite moral—one even should do it.' These were the professor's ideas, as she acknowledged by adding: 'Does he believe that? God!'

Suzanne took advantage of her parents' absence to hold a party on 25 April to which Orr came, with his wife Sadie. Suzanne was not going to give up on her professor, now that she was sure he was interested in her. Still, her ambivalence remained: 'Oh how weak people are—no self-control, but because he is weak, because no one likes him very much—that is why I must love him. But I am in such a muddle.' The day following her party she was sure that Orr had spoken directly to her in his lecture and was so overwrought she would not go to the movies with her friends: 'I am too worked up inside to sit passively and be more worked up.'

Her turbulent state continued all week, even invading her sleep. 'I dreamt that obeying moral laws were alright for ordinary people, but that I was above the law and should do what I feel is genuine.' She had to talk to him about it. On Friday she sat outside the lecture theatre until he came by. 'We talked about marriage—that one should be able to have outside relations,' and he asked if there were a sect on campus which believed in free love. Then he invited her to visit his room the next Monday. Suzanne knew this was all wrong; that she should not be enticing her weak-willed professor in this way. 'The power one has over men is rather terrifying,' she naively asserts, 'if only one could experiment without hurting others.' To her relief her parents returned from their trip away that weekend. 'I wanted

Mummy home very much ... Mummy will never do anything idiotic and will not allow me to do something silly.' Too late.

On Monday Suzanne went to her professor's room and came away in an absolutely feverish state. He had wanted to know what she was thinking; wanted to know why, if she believed it was possible to base life on genuine feeling, wouldn't she tell him. Suzanne thought he knew her thoughts and she was ashamed to voice them. 'And his eyes—they did something to me—overpowered me.' She was very confused. 'I wish everything about me was written where I could go and look up myself.' She had to see him again. The next day she deliberately went past the block where Orr was building his new house, and yes, he was there. And yes, he was pleased to see her.

The May holidays whisked Suzanne away from Hobart for two weeks but when she returned to university her infatuation was not cured. Again she went to see Orr in his room and he told her to come again at night, since he had so many meetings during the day. 'I will go of course. But why do I feel so nervous. I trust him, I do. I will.'

She went on the night of Friday 12 June. She wrote up the next day a breathless account of the experience 'in German so no-one else can read it'. At first Orr talked to her about Milanov and then he said to her: 'I like it very much sitting here with you.' She admitted she liked it too. 'And so it began. Little by little we revealed we felt an attraction for each other. Nicely and delicately—he said "you have such deep eyes the deepest I have ever seen. Sphinxlike. So peaceful, so silent." I gave him a sense of well-being.' The professor told her it was inevitable that people have crushes on their teachers and that someone had said that she had a crush on him. He felt it was his moral duty to tell her that, in case he was leading her on unconsciously, and so free her to make her own choices. But then she was a mature woman, and he could tell from her deep, questioning eyes that she was past crushes. As for himself, he had to admit he was emotionally involved. That had never happened to him before, he told her, and he didn't know where it would end. If she never wanted to visit him again he would respect her wishes, but would always love her.

Suzanne felt impelled by this honesty to tell her side: how she knew this would happen and feared she had power over him and was abusing it.

> He seemed more and more astounded, that I, so he said, had so much depth and insight ... he spoke freely to me—sometimes a little embarrassed, but spoke so much that when we said goodbye he was quite surprised that he could have said so much. It is not easy to tell a student the most important and deepest things in life. Certainly I must be very important and good for him ... I was amazed when we discovered it was 11 o'clock.

As the tumultuous evening wound up Orr asked Suzanne 'if anyone had made love to me, what did I feel? Would I feel the same if he did?' Suzanne didn't know. 'But I know that he will do it, although I don't know how far it will go.'

As is the way of these things, her parents discovered about the party held in their absence and that a married student of whom her father disapproved had been present. Her father was furious. He and Suzanne had another of their arguments. Reg Kemp was an authoritarian and overbearing man who had no grasp of his daughter's intellectual yearning. He wanted her to do as she was told, to be a conventional, good girl. Suzanne resented it. 'Fight, fight, hide, say nothing, do everything right, so that it doesn't hurt anyone. He believes I am completely without responsibility, incapable of looking after myself. And if he knew of P. Orr. My God, I can't imagine what would happen.'

The resentment and the fear of her father's reaction to her infatuation with Orr festered through the week till on Sunday she confided: 'I have fought for so long against something indefinable now I see it, as P.O. says, is my father. What right has he to decide my life and love? Why can he, who sees everything opposite from me, make me destroy my love? That is how I will hurt him. I will deny him. How can he when it is against my own ideas and feelings, make me hold myself back.' Now that Professor Orr had opened her eyes to her possibilities, and the inhibiting influence of her staid parents, caution seemed unworthy. Unlike her father, with his blind adherence to convention, 'P. Orr loves me for myself, he understands me instinctively, what I say, even what I don't say better than myself'. After all, Professor Orr had told her, 'it would be worth my whole life only to be with you here a moment and hold you in my arms. What has the outside world to do with us?' Father, mother, Mrs Orr, even her friends, were all cast aside in her dream of love.

One evening a few days later, Suzanne met Professor Orr on the post office steps, having told her parents she was going to a concert. He took her in his car to look at his house site and then suggested a drive to a secluded park at the top of Mt Nelson above the city to look at the lights of the city. 'It was beautiful ... he kissed me so softly as if he were afraid of breaking me.' Unfortunately another car came by so they went halfway down the hill to another parking spot. 'He wanted so much to love me. At first he was gentle. He had to sit on my left side. Took off his overcoat. Held me to him. Said I was beautiful. Didn't I know? He wanted to find me, bring me out of myself.' However much she may have anticipated this attention, Suzanne was a bit uptight. Why could she not relax, her professor wanted to know. 'Because I didn't love him completely? Because I thought it was wrong? Because I am incapable of being led by my feelings? Perhaps a bit of each.' By contrast he was 'hard and vital' and somewhat insistent. He asked if she wanted to begin her sexual experience with him.

> God, how can I say that? He said I did want it very much ... he held me tightly, like a man who knows

> what he is doing and what he wants ... he said I would never find anyone who would love me so much and understand me. It was not only sex this desire for me. One can, through physical contact, express something deeper than sex.

This kind of talk was just what Suzanne craved, but she wasn't ready for sexual initiation and told him not to go any further: 'I only wanted to sit and lay my head on his shoulder and that he should hold me in his strong arms.'

There were a few more night-time drives to secluded spots and bouts of what her peers would have called heavy petting—'we just touched one another'—before she could write in July: 'So it has happened and I—I am no longer a virgin.' She wasn't overwhelmed with the experience, as she may have hoped. 'I love him—yes. I cannot deny that. But my love for him will certainly not, cannot, become the highest fulfilment, the love of my life. I know that and therefore I should not look for fulfilment in physical love—sex. I should not go any further.'

But she did. In court Suzanne gave details of regular assignations at several different beaches, usually sandbanks (the professor carried a rug in his car) and once on a piece of Burnie-board at his partially completed house. In most cases they were unobserved, although 'two men and a dog' passed close by on one beach and at Bellerive beach Orr's car got stuck in a ditch and they had to go to a nearby house to get a tow. Once the university accountant saw her at the house site, even though she tried to hide. Some time after her nineteenth birthday they moved indoors to the bedroom at his home. It was, after all, the middle of winter.

When questioned about why she did not resist Orr, Suzanne said 'he did have some sort of power over me ... all through our association I held back and was talked into things by Professor Orr.' She had not intended the sexual relationship 'but I suppose I got into such a state that I thought it would be rather peculiar if I didn't or that it would be wrong or something like that.' She felt that Orr did have a powerful hold on her. She was very suggestible. Over two years of lectures she had come to identify totally with his ideas. 'His ideas on love especially influenced me,' she told the court, 'he used to say that he felt love in all its forms to be supreme and good, and whether it was expressed conventionally, that is by marriage, or outside the conventions, it was still ... the highest value in his life.' Suzanne was impressed too with the parallels Orr drew between himself and Christ. 'He said that both Christ and he were illegitimate ... that was a great burden to carry through life and Christ had overcome his through love, and I think, although he did not say it exactly, he was drawing a comparison in that respect, and imagined that he ... was overcoming his affliction by love also.' Whatever the reason, Jesus and the professor were firmly aligned in Suzanne's mind. 'I did think of Professor Orr as I thought of Christ,' she told the judge.

Suzanne was far from secure in her feelings for Orr. Her diary records several reactions of repugnance for the situation in which she found herself. In August, away from Orr on holidays, she wrote: 'I feel a sort of disgust as if I were degrading myself when I meet you at night.' Her letter from Orford displays a strong ambivalence toward him. In fact, she told the court, before Christmas she had decided not to see him any more. She had even changed her enrolment so she would not take philosophy any more. In answer to a question about whether she had ceased to be in love, she said: 'My emotions were so involved that I could not tell ... I do not think it was love at all.' The evening she spent with Orr on 23 December when he gave her a pair of marcasite earrings, was to be the last. She had not intended to visit him on her return from holidays in February, but he had rung and insisted she come and see him. Once in his house she felt the pull of his influence all over again and she was back in his bed. That uneasy situation might have continued into the academic year had not Geoffrey Allison persuaded

Suzanne to tell her parents what she was up to.

Orr had a very different tale to tell. He did not deny that Suzanne had been a very frequent visitor to his office, came often to his house and went on picnics and outings with his family. He would have been unwise to deny this, since the regularity and length of her visits to his office had been noticed by several of his colleagues and he had twice been seen having lunch with Suzanne by a member of the German department. Geoff Harrison, too, had seen Suzanne, trying to hide, with Orr at his building site. Others had seen them together in his car or with his family. Her relationship with him was the subject of persistent gossip and several people, including Jan Locher, had warned Orr not to fool around with Suzanne as it could get him into a great deal of trouble. He told these people that she was coming to talk to him about psychological problems she had at home. He also told them he would put a stop to the visits. Whether they believed him is another matter.

Essentially the explanation Orr gave to the court was that Suzanne Kemp meant no more to him than any of his other female students. He also agreed that sexual intimacy between a professor and a student was morally improper and that 'if the teacher were married it would undoubtedly complicate his capacity to carry out his duties.' However, he had not been sexually intimate with Suzanne. He denied having taken her on night drives to the various parking spots she had mentioned; denied having made love to her; denied having given her presents; denied telling her he was of royalty or comparing his situation with that of Christ. In short, he said 'these charges are a mere figment of the imagination.' In cross-examination he persistently denied giving her a pair of earrings, despite a positive identification from the jeweller, a Mr Poga, but he did admit to giving her a book for her birthday in which he had written two inscriptions: 'An unexamined life is not worth living' and, simply, 'Know thy self.' In explanation he said: 'Miss Kemp had mentioned that no-one had recognized her birthday at home and before she left my office I went to the bookshelf and picked out a book ... She was a very lonely and pathetic child.' The inscription was dated 30 September, about the time he claimed to have told her not to come so frequently to his room. He said that she had told him she was becoming 'emotionally involved' and he had repulsed her. He did not deny that after that occasion Suzanne came regularly to his house and went on outings with his family.

Orr was most emphatic in his denial that she had gone to bed with him in his house while his wife was present. Sadie Orr, as a supporting witness, agreed the suggestion was 'absurd' and that she would not have tolerated it, having then to endure intimate questions about the relationship with A. She agreed, haltingly, that in Melbourne she had tolerated a similar situation over four years. Fending off this distressing reference to the past, Mrs Orr said 'the whole thing has been such a bitter and painful experience ... the same thing could never happen in my life—never.' She saw nothing unusual in her husband's relationship with the girl: 'He has always been interested in his students.'

As to the incident in which his car got stuck near the sandbanks at Bellerive late at night, Professor Orr had an explanation. Suzanne had come to his room about 8 pm and stayed talking for about an hour. He offered to drive her home and, at her suggestion, turned and drove in the opposite direction as they continued the discussion. He drove across the river and kept driving aimlessly till the road ran out and they found themselves at the sandbanks, where they continued the discussion till 11 pm. When he tried to leave he discovered the car was stuck and both went to a nearby house to get a tow. Orr said this incident took place some time in August and gave precise details of the route he took, which was a continuation of the road over the bridge—a route which subsequent evidence showed had been blocked off since the beginning of June. To have got to the remote place where the car stuck he would have had to take a circuitous route which had no other destination than that well-known parking spot.

Neither Orr nor Suzanne Kemp could accurately date this drive, but Mr Gathercole, identified as the man who pulled the car out of the sand, was sure it was during the week 20–27 August and was confident that it was on the 25th or 26th. He was less confident who was in the car and would not identify either person, as it had been very dark. Although he was often called out on such errands, that particular car, a dark Holden, similar to that driven by Professor Orr, was the only one he pulled out during 1955. Orr was able to produce irrefutable evidence that from 22 August he was in Melbourne at a conference. Nothing in his evidence, or the evidence of Suzanne Kemp or Mr Gathercole, ruled out the likelihood that the drive happened on 20 August, before he left for Melbourne and the day after Suzanne returned from her holidays in Burnie. In any case the professor insisted the drive was quite innocent and that no sexual intimacy occurred.

For one other alleged occasion of a beach outing with Suzanne, Orr had witnesses that he was at the university. Suzanne had given evidence that on 16 December, a fortnight after Edwin Tanner's complaint to the vice-chancellor, she and Orr had gone to Kingston beach for lunch and a swim—no sex. They had left Hobart at around 11.45 and stayed at the beach 'about two hours', returning after three she thought, because Orr had to be back at the university 'because there was a council meeting and he thought he might have been dismissed.' On the return they had overtaken a bus containing a fellow academic, George Wilson, and she had to duck in order to avoid being seen. (Only one bus went over that route and it would have been passing at 2.18 pm which suggests they got back to Hobart about 2.45.) Refuting this evidence Orr insisted that he was at university all day, as would be expected given the serious events of the day, except when he went home for lunch. History lecturer Malcolm McCrae gave evidence that he had told Orr at about

11.20 am to go to his room and stay there until he was contacted. He had rung Orr between 2.30 and 3.00 and the professor had gone to McCrae's room, where they tried to telephone his legal advisor in Devonport. When this proved futile, Orr said he was going home. McCrae was able to fix this time of his meeting with Orr 'by the sequence of events that followed prior to that'. His memory may have been faulty, since the PMG department was able to prove that no calls were placed to Devonport on that day before 4.31 pm. Another witness, SRC president Malcolm Hills, swore that he met Orr at about 1.00 pm in the university grounds. Hills was with Professor Carey, with whom he shared a bottle of orangeade in the hot afternoon sun. Carey and Orr went off together for a meeting and did not return. Professor Carey, after giving the matter a great deal of thought, could not remember the sequence of events that way. He was sure that he met Orr at about 3.30 before going to the council meeting at 4.00 pm. He had asked Orr to meet him at 1.00 pm but Orr had said he had another appointment in the city. Other evidence made it clear that Orr had seen McCrae *after* that 3.30 pm meeting and not before. George Wilson did not give evidence to say whether or not he was on a bus from Kingston on the afternoon of 16 December. Despite what has been repeated *ad nauseam* on this point, Orr had no unshakeable alibi for his whereabouts between 11.20 am and 3.00 pm on 16 December when Suzanne said he was with her at the beach.

That Suzanne should have imagined an affair with her professor and translated this fantasy into diary entries made sense to Orr, if not to the judge. 'A university professor, especially of philosophy, becomes the centre of all life for a period for many sensitive students,' he explained. 'It is often a very great emotional attachment.' Added to this, Suzanne Kemp was 'a very disturbed girl'. As he had tried to explain on the occasion of the visit from her overwrought father, he had been 'increasingly disturbed by the things she had told me over the months and told her to consult a psychiatrist.' When asked 'how in the name of fortune' he could explain a female student writing to him in the terms expressed in Suzanne's letter from Orford, Orr said he had found it 'puzzling and disturbing'. The letter was open to 'certain psychological interpretation', he felt, but he was not prepared to make such interpretations himself. He agreed that he had replied, twice, to this disturbing missive, saying that he told Suzanne, in so many words, that her main difficulty was in her relationship with her father and that she must work this out. He had carefully avoided discussing her feelings for him because he was afraid of her reaction if spurned. 'The letter had alarmed me greatly. It revealed things I did not suspect. She had in her own words "deep and violent emotions".' He did not want to rouse her to vengeful responses. In fact he was 'paralysed with fear' by the letter—shocked, too, at her sacrilegious references to Christ. 'Christ is psychological, it could be very significant that anyone should think of me as Christ,' he explained, adding: 'It is not a complacent position to occupy in the mind.' The suggestion that he saw any parallels between himself and Christ was 'monstrous'; worse than her astounding claim that he claimed to be royalty. He would never have said anything so patently ridiculous.

Nor did he agree that he had asked Suzanne to destroy the letters he had written to her, clearly recalling that she had told him of destroying the letters because his response had made her so angry. But Suzanne did not speak of any hot-headed response to Orr's letters, only that Orr had rebuked her for not knowing the true meaning of love; and said that she could not love him properly if she based it on needing him. He had expounded on this theme for some pages, she said, before complaining about his builders and his job. 'He said he had enough worries at the university and at the house without me worrying him more.' His second letter was sent because she had not replied to the first and reiterated the message in 'a long psychological description of the ins and outs of loving'.

Suzanne did not believe that Orr had ever told her to go to a psychiatrist, although she agreed her talks with him had plenty of psychological analysis, since Orr was very taken with psychology. But she had not sought him out for counselling: 'we were just talking as far as I was concerned.' For his part Orr insisted she came to him with deep-seated personal problems related to her family and her relationships with people in general. Attempting to help her, he had told her that 'the significant thing, as she herself often remarked, was the relationship with her father.' He said she felt that her father did not love her; that he was brutal toward her, and that this created serious psychological problems for her. Orr had advised her often, advice he says he repeated in his letters to her, to 'go to your father and tell him that you feel unloved. Tell him that, instead of being antagonistic toward him break down and let him know your feeling, and until your relationship with your father is righted, all your emotional relationship in life will be distorted.' He had urged her to see a psychiatrist to work through the problem with her father. This was news to Suzanne, although, at the earlier inquiry she had described discussions with Orr concerning her family: 'I daresay I criticized my parents and I don't suppose it is abnormal if you do. He drew comparisons I would never have thought of myself ... we had a lot of psychological discussions about myself, and about other people he had known, forcing me to draw comparisons ... it got around to [my family] and he made me think that I was abnormal ... that the actions of my father proved he did not love me ... I must have said something in the beginning.'

Orr said he had been convinced that Suzanne's father held the key to her strange destructive fantasy about himself. After all, it was Reginald Kemp, not his daughter, who had made a complaint against him, when only days earlier Suzanne, against her father's wishes, had written a letter to say her relationship with her professor was perfectly proper. And, more significantly, she had written another letter to say her father was restraining her.

In court Orr repeated that he had told Kemp it was his brutality which caused Suzanne's psychological problems. However, he did not repeat his allusion to sexual impropriety between father and daughter, even though Reginald Kemp repeated the allegation (in a confidential note handed to the judge) during his evidence.[84] In a document written after the Supreme Court case and entitled 'Why She Should Frame Him', Orr elaborated his concerns about father and daughter. In his interpretation 'it would require an unusually powerful and uncommon motive to account for the fact that a wealthy and aspiring socialite should so obviously destroy her own reputation.'[85] But the real puzzle for Orr was why Reginald Kemp should have forced her to expose herself to ridicule and vulgar comment. It seemed obvious that Kemp was protecting himself, not his daughter, but in the document Orr only hinted at a 'more earthy reason' as to why Suzanne's father would be in need of protection. This was a theme that Orr was to develop and refine in the years to come, but before Justice Green he was not prepared to be drawn beyond vague references to Reginald Kemp's lack of affection for his supposedly disturbed daughter.

There is something very familiar in Orr's insistence that Suzanne had psychological problems stemming from her family. In his *Pix* articles he had said much the same thing about A, saying that she was disturbed by the unhealthy influence of an overbearing mother. Then Edwin Tanner, after complaining about Orr, was also said to be psychologically distressed. Orr claimed that Tanner, like Suzanne, had come to see him to discuss 'personal, psychological and professional difficulties'. (When Tanner discovered that Orr had told his colleagues that he 'was cracking up' he had not taken this seriously since Orr had also said that his architect had an inferiority complex, but he had become more concerned when it was apparent that Orr had been telling people that he had been in the mental institution at New Norfolk.)

Even though Orr's entire case hinged on Suzanne having

been in a deranged state, he was unable to produce anyone who could confirm that she had a neurosis about her home life, or testify to her desperate unhappiness or 'violent emotions'. Suzanne's demeanour during nearly four days of gruelling cross-examination did not suggest any instability. The press consistently remarked on her composure and what *Truth* described as 'amazing self-possession which few women could equal'. Nor, despite his private opinions about Suzanne's sexual activities, could he produce anybody with whom she might have visited the parking spots she described with such unerring accuracy. There were students who gave evidence in support of Orr's character, but not to the detriment of Suzanne's character. One student witness, Patricia Ure, giving evidence in support of Orr, told the court how he had invited her, on one occasion, to go up Mt Wellington 'to see the lights of Hobart'. She had refused. Several of these student witnesses were very surprised to find, when gathered together in a room below the Supreme Court, that Orr's lawyers intended to challenge the Kemp allegations, rather than argue this was a personal, not professional, matter. Until that moment Jan Locher had believed that the defence would be based on the Haldane case in the 1920s, when a prominent academic at Cambridge had been sacked for an adulterous relationship but had successfully fought for reinstatement on the grounds that his personal relationship had no bearing on his professional conduct.[86]

Professor Orr's assertions about Suzanne's mental health was a double-edged sword. While he could tell the judge that he had suggested that Suzanne see a psychiatrist, he was forced to admit that he himself had been consulting a psychiatrist. Moreover, a string of witnesses were able to give examples of behaviour from the professor which was distinctly bizarre, if not downright nutty. Professor Townsley's wife told how Orr had kept their house under surveillance during the royal commission and how he would harass them with wordless phone calls at all hours of night. Her husband claimed Orr had threatened him in a 'sinister' fashion, saying that Townsley was 'lucky something had not happened to him'. Suzanne, as well as Milanov and Tanner, told how the professor had spoken about his prestigious but tragic birth, while weeping uncontrollably. This story about being related to royalty, was, according to Orr 'complete fantasy. Nothing remotely approaching this has occurred.' Nevertheless, his old comrades Professor Carey and Associate Professor Polya both gave evidence that he had told them he was the illegitimate son of the Duke of Windsor. Any number of other colleagues could have confirmed this delusion. They may even have provided some levity by reciting a limerick on the subject:

A lunatic prof known as Orr
Declared his own mother a whore
From the fantastic themes
Of his Freudian dreams
He deduced that his père was Windsor[87]

There is a lot more that could be said about Professor Orr's disingenuousness in court, but I don't intend to labour the point.

Much has been made of the use of Orr's dreams in the court. Eddy saw this as the ultimate proof of the black depths to which the Tasmanian legal system had sunk, when a man's dreams could be used against him. Other less histrionic claims suggest that the record of Orr's dreams, subpoenaed from Milanov, created an atmosphere which made charges against Orr credible. It is true that Reg Wright made references to Orr's dreams when questioning him about his royal connections, but it was Orr himself who insisted that the dream records be tabled in court to prove they were not riddled with references to royal parentage. From that point Orr's subconscious associations were fair game as far as Wright was concerned. The judge saw otherwise, explicitly informing the court that he would neither read the record of dreams nor attempt to put any interpretation on them.

The transcript of the Supreme Court case and the supporting documents are available in the High Court archives and the Melbourne University archives, along with a transcript of the appeal. Should anyone think I am loading the dice against Orr, they might like to read them. Having read them carefully, I agree with Justice Green that 'Suzanne Kemp is telling the truth while the plaintiff is not.' This is not to say that Suzanne was entirely consistent or that she did not make mistakes about times and places remembered from some eighteen months earlier. Nor would I want to deny that she was eager to initiate a relationship with her professor and was 'passing through a period of turbulent eroticism'. But there is no doubting the substance of her evidence concerning the nature of her relationship with Orr—a relationship he emphatically denied and equally forcefully said was improper. Professor Orr never once argued that he should not be dismissed if the allegations against him were true. It seems to me, therefore, that whatever we may think about the matter nowadays, the university was quite within its rights to dismiss Orr. I am also inclined to echo the justices of the High Court and express surprise than anyone would think differently.

CHAPTER SIX

Since the days of Potiphar's wife, many an innocent man has been ruined

There were those who thought differently. Curiously, one was Roy Douglas Wright, the brother of the university's barrister, Senator Reg Wright. Universally known by his nickname 'Panzee' (short for 'chimpanzee'), equally for his homely features, burly frame and awesome temper, professor of physiology at Melbourne, vice-president of the Council for Civil Liberties, and a well-known champion of left—liberal causes, he was the driving force behind the staff association at Melbourne, a university to which he was passionately committed and of which he became chancellor in later life. Panzee became a professor in 1938 when he was only thirty-one, and by 1958 was a larger-than-life figure in Melbourne intellectual circles, either adored or reviled, depending on one's political colour. He was described by one male journalist as both caveman and genius; while another woman journalist noted that he had as much use for charm as a bear has for perfume.

Having turned his back on Tasmania when he went to Melbourne to finish his medical degree, Panzee developed an offhand contempt for the 'parochial xenophobic community'[88] he left behind. It was fashionable to denigrate Tasmania then, as it still is in some quarters. Academics, conscious of their peripheral status in the intellectual community which revolved around England, took comfort in being able to sneer at a place even more peripheral than Melbourne or Sydney. Throughout his life, Panzee enjoyed an amicable sparring relationship with his brother Reg which often found them very pointedly on opposite sides of the fence. These two were the last of a large rural family from the Tasmanian north-west, and unlike their siblings they had gone to university rather than stay on the land. Rivalry between them was fierce. They were very much alike physically, yet poles apart politically and intellectually. Panzee was disappointed in his brother's narrow Tasmanian focus and had scant regard for the practice of law, while Reg found Panzee's exaltation of 'the community of scholars' absurdly pompous. They were as alike as two bookends, Reg's daughter said, and they died within weeks of each other.

It is part of the mythology about the Orr case that Panzee and Reg Wright fought out their sibling rivalry over Orr, and the idea is not without some foundation, but it does little justice to Panzee's extraordinary crusading zeal in defence of the principle of academic freedom and an open society. As he saw it, the dismissal of Orr posed a serious threat to these things he valued so highly. Once alerted to the danger he was prepared to invest large amounts of time and money, as well as prodigious amounts of energy, in defending the disgraced professor.

Orr first approached Panzee Wright after the failure of his High Court appeal in May 1957. As he recalls, Orr came to see him with an ex-colleague from Melbourne. 'I saw it, as explained to me in those moments, as an assault on the institution of a university—you know, a University *qua* University,' which was not, by implication, a place like the Hobart institution run by 'a bunch of yokels' who had 'set about destroying an energetic academic'. To Orr he was characteristically direct, saying '"Well, let's face it, did you do it?" He said "No, Panz, I didn't."' This declaration was sufficient, it seems, for Panzee to vigorously enter the fray. Throughout his life he insisted that the decision to support Orr was purely a matter of principle: 'It wasn't that I liked Orr, I always regarded him as a bit of a twit, actually.'[89]

Panzee agreed to take on the rather arcane legal position of 'next friend' to Orr, once he had established to his own satisfaction certain points of principle. 'I told him that my view was that a professor who seduced one of his students should be dismissed. He agreed with me. I further told him if I detected him in any untruth I would not further help him.'[90] Panzee believed academics had the same professional responsibility toward students that doctors had toward their patients. During his protracted period as Orr's public defender Panzee claimed to have made rigorous and extensive inquiries into Orr's conduct at his previous universities and was satisfied that his record was impeccable. It later transpired that he had only sighted testimonials from friendly academics in the United Kingdom.

Once Panzee had committed himself, Orr was in turn committed to a defence which totally repudiated Suzanne Kemp. He was forced to reject the argument advanced by philosophers from Sydney University, who also gave him support, that sex between student and teacher was strictly a private matter. Although counsel for Orr had made this argument before the High Court, it was a position that Panzee would not tolerate. He was displeased by the actions of Professor Alan Stout of Sydney University, who had alerted the international academic community to the denial of natural justice and carried the torch for Orr's cause over the previous year. Stout was most concerned with the principle of natural justice and the master—servant relationship, and was not prepared to publicly state that Orr was innocent of the Kemp charge, admitting in his *Ama* article that there was 'no plausible explanation as to why Miss Kemp should have invented her story'. Panzee did not acknowledge Stout's several articles promoting Orr's case. 'If I did,' he wrote to Orr, 'It would be to ask him if I ever got into trouble please not to try and help me.'[91] Both Panzee and Orr were confident they had plausible reasons for Suzanne's lying about her professor, and they set about compiling their evidence and looking for a forum at which to air it.

In the previous year Orr had been casting his net widely in the hope of getting influential people to rally to his cause. Attempts to interest the Australian Council for Cultural Freedom (ACCF) had fallen foul of the president, Sir John Latham, a close friend of Sir John Morris, who believed the issue had been decided decisively by the court. Influential members of ACCF were not so sure. James McAuley, visiting Hobart in December 1956 at the invitation of the new Archbishop, Guildford Young, got the full treatment from Orr, along with his lawyer friend Hal Wootten. They spent an entire night, till dawn, listening to Orr talk without cease with 'tremendously intense glittering eyes'. As Wootten remembers it, Orr 'told this horrific story about a disturbed girl who had framed him'. He was disconcerted by Orr's exulted rave about the wonderful relationship with A in Melbourne, all the while quite impervious to the obvious distress of his silent, weeping wife. McAuley likewise remembers Orr's intensity (and insensitivity), and how 'his account was organized so it would have maximum appeal to what he would regard as my special interests.' Prominent lawyer John Kerr was recruited to help Hal Wootten review the Supreme Court evidence and make a case to the ACCF, where there was now great pressure 'to jump on the Orr bandwagon'. Reading the transcript, Wootten was quick to realise that 'Orr told me a pack of lies about the court proceeding' while McAuley was equally upset that 'things Orr said on the night were not in accordance with what came out in the transcript, and parts of it rather sickened us because his account of certain matters, in the presence of his wife, was in contradiction to what was dragged out of Mrs Orr in Court.' In the meantime, McAuley had been receiving regular phone calls from Orr: 'I had become part of the network of Orr supporters and from a distance, the way in which things would be pitched, the way the line would be run in a way that would appeal to me, began to come out. I began to feel I was being manipulated.' Each of them concluded they had been conned. 'In a sense we became anti-Orr because of a sense of distrust, of a sense that this was a liar and a very clever con man.'[92] So the ACCF did not become an ally in the Orr cause.

There were others within the staff association at Sydney

University and especially among the Association of Philosophers who continued to believe that Orr had suffered injustice of some sort. These included Ted Wheelwright and Ken Buckley, who were key players in the emergent FCUSA. They all had some doubt about Orr's denial of the Kemp charge, but this was overridden by a strong feeling that Tasmania was a strange, class-ridden and backward place ruled by a nineteenth-century oligarchy whose members would flout and pervert the law if it suited them. Essentially these were men of the left, but they saw no political dimension in the case. For them the overriding issue in the Orr case was the establishment of the royal commission. Orr had been punished, they believed, for his part in forcing university reforms. They were surprised to find themselves joined by Harry Eddy, 'who saw reds under every bed and conspiracies everywhere,' and Ted Wheelwright was 'amazed when he introduced a political dimension.'[93] Harry Eddy was to be Orr's most voluble and longest-lasting defender. During 1957 he began writing a book which he believed would bring the true issues in the Orr case to the world.

In Hobart too there were new allies drawn into the Orr campaign, especially an ABC announcer, Paul Berry, who saw in the Orr case echoes of his own unhappy experiences with the legal system, especially with Stanley Burbury, who had denied him a divorce. It was Burbury's handiwork he detected in the 'illogicality and rationalization of patent untruth' of Green's judgement. Something of a bush lawyer with a reputation for being litigious, he became a staunch supporter of Orr not because 'of a predisposition toward him as a person but because of my growing revulsion and concern at the things which appeared to pass as normal practice in the law in Tasmania.'[94] Not that Orr was without support in the corridors of power. One long-standing member of parliament was doing a great job, Orr reported to Panzee, denouncing Suzanne as 'a psychopathic bitch ... mad as her grandmother ever was'. Thankfully Suzanne had left town soon after the court case, leaving Orr to lament 'la Kemp is still celebrated throughout the town as holidaying in luxury in Europe.'[95]

Despite enthusiastic moral support, Panzee and Orr felt stymied with no further recourse to the courts. Preferring to ignore the advice from law professors Derham, Sawyer and Neary that the Green judgement stood up well to legal scrutiny, Orr wrote to Stout about the need for an inquiry 'where we could bring out the "motive" the Kemps had and bring in the psychiatrists.'[96] He had already bombarded Stout, currently preparing an article, with his evidence that the diary had been forged. Stout was pivotal to Orr's campaign because of his impeccable moral standing in the intellectual community. Orr understood that if Stout could be got to put the case in his stead, few would question its authenticity.

It was Paul Berry, a member of the Presbyterian Church for a time, who suggested Orr make an application for readmittance to the Scots Kirk (his membership having lapsed) and have the ecclesiastical court 'try' him all over again. Should the Kirk decide Orr was the victim of justice miscarried, the moral authority of the church would give great weight to his case. The enthusiastic new moderator of the Scots Kirk, Hector Dunn, was agreeable to this manoeuvre, having been won over to the Orr cause. In February 1958 Berry formally asked the session to extend fellowship to the disgraced professor. Orr and his allies set about gathering 'new evidence' to disprove Suzanne's story in her absence.

In December 1957 Orr's letters to Stout mention even more new evidence and hint at momentous revelations as to the Kemps' 'motive'. Here for the first time is the reference to a supposed psychiatrist from Launceston, Dr Engisch. In January 1958 Orr gives further details of his new evidence; the jeweller, Mr Poga, who said he sold Orr the earrings Suzanne produced in court was now willing to say he didn't and 'was inveigled into giving evidence'; a reputable citizen 'on hearing for the first time about the earrings' had come forward to swear that he saw Mr

Kemp buy the earrings; Suzanne's letter from Orford is shown to be a neurotic fabrication; and from Dr Engisch—something even better.[97]

Orr was running ahead of himself, since he had not got this evidence but was only putting it together. That in itself was an intriguing process. Take the matter of the earrings. In December 1957 Orr paid a visit to Poga in his jeweller's shop and sent a lengthy account to his lawyer claiming that Poga 'admitted very frankly and apologetically that he had made a mistake in his identification.' He further admitted, said Orr, that he had sold them to Geoff Allison and that he had been forced to give evidence by Kemp and Allison. Orr was very happy with this evidence, for it confirmed what he had suspected, that Allison was a prime mover in a conspiracy against him.[98] The next day he was unable to get a statutory declaration from Poga to this effect. Many phone calls later Poga would still not put on paper what Orr claims to have been told. On 20 January Orr received a statement from the 'reputable citizen' who claimed to have been in the shop when Allison bought the earrings. This man was none other than Paul Berry. Another statement followed from a student supporter, MS Graham, who had previously been writing letters to Stout to say there were 'strong reasons for doubting [Suzanne's] emotional and mental stability'.[99] Graham claimed that Poga had said someone other than Orr had purchased the earrings with Suzanne. In the next few months Orr and others made visits to the jeweller's home and his shop without eliciting a statement. On the other hand, following a query from the university lawyer, Poga had reiterated his absolute belief that Orr had bought these earrings and that Orr was pestering him to say otherwise. He did not bear Orr any grudge, he explained, but the facts were the facts. The failure of Poga to actually swear to his supposed perjury was not communicated to Stout, busily publishing pro-Orr articles in Sydney, and perhaps he did not see the small item in the Hobart press, just before the Scots Kirk held its inquiry in June, reporting that Poga sought police protection. According to the *Mercury*, the jeweller claimed to have been receiving anonymous and abusive phone calls at all hours of the night and was being harassed by people associated with Orr constantly calling at his shop.

What is most intriguing about this cloak-and-dagger activity was that Orr's counsel had actually conceded the point about the earrings at the appeal eight months earlier. Had Orr forgotten? When Justice Taylor pointed out that Suzanne ran a great risk in saying Orr gave her the earrings, counsel for Orr said:

> they are only a pair of trumpery trinkets when all is said and done—she dined there and so on; Professor and Mrs Orr had been invited to a party at her home, and she had been given the earrings as a Christmas gift and they [the Orrs] very foolishly decided to deny it. Here is a professor that has grave charges against him, and so on and he thinks to himself 'Well I have given her earrings—the wife and I have given her earrings—it will be most damaging to our case' and it would go very much to his credit in that regard that he told the lie.

Since Justice Taylor did not seem to care, Orr's counsel concluded the matter of earrings was 'so trivial that I need not worry about it'. Apparently it was not trivial to whoever was ringing Mr Poga in the wee small hours.

The members of the Scots Kirk, who were unanimously impressed with Orr's truthfulness, decided that the earrings were no mere trifle but a 'means used to commit a fraud upon the court'.[100] When he finally got his mammoth book together over two years later, Harry Eddy gave the earrings much prominence, devoting a whole chapter to Poga in which he refers to 'alleged criminal activity' but says that he is not at liberty to use the relevant evidence.

Other items of 'new evidence' are just as suspect. Much was

made, again, of Orr's whereabouts on 16 December to prove he was not at Kingston beach. Statements were tendered from two students who had remembered having a meeting with Professor Orr during the crucial hours. One student was Manu Bunnag whose statement was sent from Thailand where he was living. The second statement also came from thousands of miles away. This was from John Biggs, who also remembered a meeting with Orr now that he was a postgraduate student in England. Interestingly, John Biggs had not remembered that meeting when he gave evidence in support of Orr at the Supreme Court. It is worth considering the evidence he did give at that time. John Biggs admitted under cross-examination that he had been very close to Orr in 1955 and had organised students in his support. Following the dismissal he went to Orr's house at least once a week to help with organising the defence. When asked about his relationship with Orr, Biggs said: 'I have done my best over a long period to try and contribute my own piece to what I thought might be the truth of the matter.' On that occasion the truth of the matter did not include a meeting with Orr at midday on 16 December. John Biggs, now a professor in Hong Kong, tells me that his memory was prompted 'around December to January 1956–57' when he arranged for Dr Engisch, a family friend, to hypnotise Orr. Using automatic writing Orr had been able to reconstruct the events of 16 December, including his lunchtime meetings.[101]

In his statement for the Kirk, Malcolm Hills reiterated, with emphatic detail, his account of a meeting with Orr and Professor Carey at 1.00 pm on that day.[102] Now this claim of Hills has always troubled me, as he was a serious-minded student unlikely to tailor the facts, so it was with particular interest that I listened to Hills' reminiscence of his involvement with the university, taped over two decades later, shortly before his premature death. On the tape Hills vividly recalls the day and describes the location, the weather, the orangeade he shared with Professor Carey with almost cinematic recall. All the elements are the same except one. On this occasion he says: 'it was about 3.00 pm in the afternoon. Certainly about an hour before the Council meeting. Orr came walking down from where he had parked his car looking very agitated and wearing dark glasses.' Orr and Carey then went away together and 'I stood waiting for him until the Council meeting. Carey never came back. I went into the Council meeting and Carey wasn't there but he came scurrying in.'[103] This account is quite in line with the account given by Professor Carey and, I hardly need add, that of Suzanne Kemp.

Not only was Orr writing to Stout about this supposedly devastating 'new evidence'; so too was Emeritus Professor Miller, enthusing that Orr had 'effective alibis against Kemp evidence' and had exposed the earrings as 'very near a Kemp conspiracy'. But Miller recognised that these would scarcely reinstate the professor of philosophy. 'Poor Orr clutches at any straw, but the straws are only illusion.'[104] Panzee Wright too realised that for a credible counter-case they had to establish a coherent motive for concocting a case against Orr. He turned his attention to the girl witness who had told these lies against his friend and the judge who had believed them.

Dealing with the judge was relatively straightforward. Justice Green was the subject of rumours about his personal life which Panzee exploited to the full. Writing to the Association of University Teachers in England he described Green as 'a bachelor in his middle fifties who lives with his mother and interests himself greatly in boys' clubs'.[105] To Eddy he pointed out an amusing typing error: 'I'm sure Dr Freud would appreciate your calling His Honour Miss Justice Green.'[106] In print he was no less direct, drawing attention to Justice Green's unmarried status, his attachment to his mother and his fostering of boys' clubs. The inference was quite explicit: His Honour was not a man who knew anything about women. There was, as well, an implicit inference to be drawn, as it was consistently in Panzee's private correspondence, that Green was open to blackmail by powerful men who wanted him to give a certain kind of judgement on Orr. Green was distressed by these descriptions of himself and spoke to his close friend Bill Hodgman about them, suggesting Hodgman try to moderate Panzee's enthusiasm. 'I might as well have tried to divert a charging elephant as try and have any influence on Panzee's behaviour' was Hodgman's reply.[107]

Suzanne Kemp's behaviour was more problematic. Here the professor of physiology was indefatigable in his efforts to get to the bottom of the matter. He caused amused speculation about the nature of his morning mail following his assertion that the Orford letter 'reminds me very strongly of letters I have received from students ... when they were under the influence of analgesic drugs.'[108] Copies of her diary and her letters were sent to forensic experts he knew around the world, to test whether they were forgeries, or written under the influence of drugs, or both. Scotland Yard and the Home Office Forensic Science Laboratory were able to confirm that all Suzanne's letters, including those pro-Orr, were written by the same hand. Nor could they detect any suggestion of drugs or coercion. He scoured psychological text books for a description of Suzanne's 'condition', copying out from Feuchel the following: 'a state of pseudological behaviour—revenge for having been deceived about sexual matters—hysterical pseudological fantastica ... hysterical characters are inclined to sexualize all non-sexual relations, irrational emotional outbreaks, chaotic behaviour dramatization and histrionic behaviour toward mendacity'.[109] There he had it! It remained for him to find a qualified psychiatrist to confirm Suzanne's condition from reading her diary. He approached a number of psychiatrists (but not those who had been treating Professor Orr), including Rose Rothfield, a woman psychoanalyst. 'We all thought the world of Panzee,' she told me, 'and probably would have done anything for him.'[110] She agreed to analyse the diary and concluded Suzanne was 'a girl of high intelligence but emotionally immature, rather like an adolescent'. Rothfield felt she had ambivalent relationships, was narcissistic and showed no evidence of capacity to love as a grown woman would. But she concluded 'I do not think Suzanne Kemp is psychotic. She herself is aware of what is false and what is not.'[111] This was not what Panzee wanted. Closer to home he found a postgraduate student in psychopharmacy who had no clinical experience with people. This young man wrote out for the Scots Kirk a detailed analysis of Suzanne's diary showing her to display signs of 'hysterical pseudologia phantastica'.[112] The psychological evidence mightily impressed the members of the Kirk, who found Suzanne's behaviour 'understandable' and Professor Orr's behaviour toward her to be 'considerate and understanding'. In less polite language Orr's parliamentary defender had said the same ... Suzanne was 'a psychotic bitch'. As Harry Eddy was to pointedly remind his readers, this was an archetype with which men were only too familiar. Throughout history hysterical women had made false charges against men 'and since the days of Potiphar's wife, many an innocent man has been ruined by them.' Only recently a nominee for the US Supreme Court had the same problem.

Orr had been less successful in getting further evidence of Suzanne's supposed psychological state. Despite his probing, no students seemed willing to say that they had found her behaviour neurotic. He had been working on a woman described as 'a psychiatric social worker in the same class as la Kemp' to say that Suzanne 'had home problems more psychiatric than social'. She refused, causing Orr to fume to Panzee: 'she is a frustrated old maid nearing forty and so open to attack.'[113] His so-called psychiatrist, Dr Engisch, also proved more difficult than anticipated. In his letters to Panzee, Orr described how Engisch had remembered, with some prompting, that he had visited Orr in March 1956 and they had discussed Suzanne. But he was 'playing coy' about making a statement. Panzee sympathised, given his own problems in getting statements from psychiatrists. They were all neurotics as far as he could see.

Orr had told Stout the previous year that he had evidence

that he had sent Suzanne to a psychiatrist and he was getting pretty desperate by March 1958 to get that evidence. He did get a statement from Engisch, on 18 March, though, once again, it was less than he might have hoped. Engisch said that in December 1955 a male student Orr had referred to him, whom he had been treating for a personality disorder (even though he worked in Launceston) told him 'that Orr was very anxious for me to treat a girl, if he could persuade her to come. I am not sure of the exact date I learnt the name of this girl was Suzanne Kemp.' He went on to say that he had visited Orr in a professional capacity after his dismissal and Orr had showed him a copy of the Orford letter and asked for an opinion of her mental state. 'I declined to give an opinion, suggesting he consult a recognized psychiatrist.'[114] This statement carried weight with the Kirk, even though it was entirely *ex post facto* reasoning and Engisch had not named the male student who carried the all-important message. Some years later he did name this student: John Biggs, who was, conveniently, still in England. When I asked John Biggs about these events he was surprised, assuring me that 'I recommended Orr to Engisch' in late 1956 or early 1957. Dr Engisch, Biggs informed me, was a GP and family friend with an interest in hypnosis. The last time Biggs was a patient was when he was eleven—Engisch removed his appendix: 'If Orr recommended a male student to Engisch then it definitely wasn't me ... my impression was that Orr didn't know Engisch at this stage.' Biggs had 'no recollection' of any discussion about Suzanne Kemp and was puzzled to find he had been cast in this pivotal role during his absence in England.[115]

In England also was Suzanne Kemp. Maybe, reasoned Orr, away from her father he could get her to recant. For this job Panzee recruited John Montrose from Queen's University at Belfast, who had lent some weight to the cause because of his deep concern about the master—servant relationship. It was the principle that mattered, he explained, regardless of what he might have heard about Orr at his old alma mater. In dealing with Montrose, Panzee had 'judged it best not to tell him what had gone on here. He seemed a nice old chap but hardly the person to handle any tough discussions.'[116] Anyway, Montrose agreed to meet Suzanne Kemp and gain her confidence. In January he sent a letter describing his achievements. He had taken some time to gain her confidence, aware that he 'had to act honourably throughout', and he was able to tell Orr, privately, that she 'showed sympathy for your plight and I am hopeful that she will write to the university asking them to behave decently toward you.' Otherwise, Montrose reported, she did not accept any suggestion of fabrication and was 'strangely calm in her denials'.[117]

In a terse letter Panzee rebuked Montrose for his qualms about using 'what Miss Kemp had said was confidential.' He wanted a statement that could be tendered as evidence. 'I trust you will recognize that I am not dealing with members of a gentlemen's club, it is essentially an agricultural community with a parliament and judiciary based on family, money and custom.'[118] To Orr he exploded about Montrose's 'naivety' and warned him against choosing as his allies people such as Montrose and Stout. Under a barrage of pressure Montrose did turn his account of the meeting with Suzanne into a statement for the Kirk: 'having been assured that in the circumstances there is nothing improper ... though at the time the understanding with Miss Kemp was that I, personally, would not make any disclosure'. He said that she told him she 'could not tie herself down to a precise date' for her visit to Kingston beach, but no more.[119]

Having failed to get a recantation from her, Orr was still very confident about his evidence against Suzanne. Her diary, he decided was a patent forgery. As well as himself, his allies Berry, Panzee, Eddy and even Stout had a go at analysing it. By comparing the transcripts of the university inquiry and the Supreme Court hearing they were able to show that the content of the diary had changed substantially between the two events.

Orr and Panzee poured hours of time and reams and reams of paper into this analysis. Writing to Stout in February 1958, Orr was insistent that in his articles Stout 'drive home that there is documentary proof that the diary is faked'.[120]

In his analysis of the diary for the Kirk, Orr points out such anomalies as an entry for June: 'between the two events the account had grown from 125 words to over 1000 words ... nearly all the material which His Honour finds significant and compromising is completely absent from the 125 words in the university version'.[121] And so on. The Kirk was horrified, decrying the 'very substantial alterations, additions and deletions' which occur in the diary on different occasions. A fraud in the court, manufactured evidence, a psychologically unstable witness and affidavits that Orr was not where Suzanne said he was, all convinced the Kirk that Orr had definitely suffered from a gross miscarriage of justice. Nothing convinced them of this more profoundly than that forged/altered/rewritten diary.

Stout's readers in Sydney were likewise shocked at such blatant manufacturing of evidence. Once it was revealed, the forged diary became a cornerstone in the Orr defence and Eddy made enormous use of it, giving thirty-one pages to exploring the inconsistencies. He had no doubt. Whoever wrote the diary 'it was forged, ie concocted as evidence against Orr.' In his television appearance on 'Meet the Press' on 15 June 1958, Orr asserts that 'scientific and legal investigation' (by which he meant the analysis of Panzee and Berry) had shown the diary produced in court was 'a very different document' to the original diary produced at the university inquiry. Not only that, 'the original diary does not contain any record or suggestion of any misconduct or impropriety on my part.'

In none of the supposedly scholarly analysis of the diary did any man make the basic point that the diary was largely written in German and had been translated for the court. They failed to state that Suzanne had initially provided a rough, oral translation direct from the loose-leaf binder and that she was acutely embarrassed and cut her translation down to its bare bones, thereby excluding any direct reference to sexual intercourse. Moreover, the diary was sighted by Orr lawyers before the trial, they agreed to a court-approved translation of it and they did not object to its being admitted as evidence. During the case the original was several times sighted to enable comparison with the typescript translation. In Hodgman's law office at the time was an associate who spoke fluent German and who made his own rough translation of the diary. He had no doubts about its authenticity. Nor, in the endless comparison of times and dates, do these scholars point out that Suzanne had not dated her entries and that the respective lawyers had agreed to a list of dates for the translated typescript, worked out from actual events described. Naturally the court diary is different to Suzanne's rough oral account. In any case the idea that some middle-aged man, possibly the vice-chancellor, concocted this piece of confused adolescent eroticism is farcical.

Panzee was prepared to use the diary in whatever way suited his purpose. While he was adamant that it was a forgery and the work of Orr's enemies, he also went through it with a fine-tooth comb looking for evidence of Suzanne's promiscuity. In a document headed 'Suzanne and the Boys' he detailed every mention of other males in the diary (presuming, I guess, that these bits were not concocted). He was also very interested in every reference to her father. Panzee was convinced that the boys mentioned probably accounted for her trips to various parking spots she described, and that one (he spent some time trying to track him down) had been with her at Bellerive and had been pulled out of the sand by Mr Gathercole. Panzee was a medical man and he knew that since Suzanne was not *virgo intacta* at the time of her complaint, some man must be responsible—someone other than Orr, that is. In this speculation he was in good company.

Stories about Suzanne's promiscuity spread like wildfire in her absence and they can still be unearthed quite readily. A description that some Orr supporters liked to use of 'Suzy', as they called her, was as 'the town bike'. 'If you knew Suzy, like I know Suzy, oh, oh oh what a girl.' The editor of *Meanjin* had been told by a well-appointed military man in Hobart that Suzanne was often seen coming and going from the military barracks and it was also said that she was equally intimate with the officers on the *Taroona* which ran between Hobart and Melbourne. And so forth. Quite remarkable, really, for a girl who was not allowed out after eleven o'clock and who was a hard-working, high-distinction student. But these stories certainly caught the intellectual imagination. In 1958 'an amusing ballad' began to circulate which has been attributed to poet and academic Bob Brissenden, in a light-hearted mood:

> Come, all you men of learning, and a warning take from me,
> I'll have you quit night-lecturing and shun Philosophy,
> and whene'er those little student girls come knocking on your door,
> Ere it's too late, think of the fate, of bold young Sydney Orr.
>
> He was born and bred in Belfast Town, and there took his degree;
> But soon he left old Ireland to sail the stormy sea;
> Transported to Van Diemen's Land, like many men before,
> He made his name, and soon became: Professor Sydney Orr.
>
> In Hobart Town this daring youth commenced his wild career,
> In the cause of Justice, Light and Truth, no foeman did he fear;
> He bailed up the pundits, and he made the Council roar;
> 'For Academic Liberty I'll live and die,' cried Orr.

And bold Sydney won his battle—the Council stood at bay
But as he pressed them strongly, his colleagues slipped away;
They left him all out in the cold; they left his backbone bare
To rumour and ridicule and every sort of snare.

Their blood boiled high, their ire rose, it was most fiery;
Until to their delight they came upon a Diary;
Like brave Parnell, and Samson whose locks Delilah shore,
A woman soon appeared who ruined poor young Sydney Orr.

They expected him, all bruised and torn, to crawl away and die,
but Sydney yelled 'Damblast them all, I'll have another try;
They put the frame around me, but I do not fit the frame—
I'll call on other Uni Dons to help get back my name.'

The Presbytery retried his case and found him white as snow,
The Profs. from other Shops yelled out: 'Give the bloke a go!'
The Council snarled and whimpered and started loud to curse,
For what they thought was bloody good had turned out bloody worse!

There's a moral to this story of the wild Colonial Don—
If you irritate the bourgeoisie you'll sure be sat upon;
But if you feel you must give voice, go get a decent mob,
Alone you'll do your sugar, your nameplate and your job![122]

Panzee also tried his hand at a ditty, which began 'Suzy told the teacher and the teacher told the Head / that Syddy stole some butter and spread it on his bread.' His literary gifts were not really equal to it. He did write a novel a few years later, equally unsuccessful as a literary endeavour, which is a very thinly disguised account of the Orr case. Should anyone have any doubts, he actually supplied a table identifying each of his characters with a protagonist in the Orr saga. His portrait of Suzanne, as of every other player, not the least himself, is revealing. 'She had never solved the Oedipus situation properly ... she was most unhappy.' Hilda, as she is called, was keen on Professor Stork (Orr), a very high-minded character, who had gently rebuffed her, but she had also been intimate with a cunning class upstart named Brown (Allison), who was working for the vice-chancellor and wanted to get Hilda and her fortune as 'damaged goods'. He had drugged her and forced her to tell her father she had been having an affair with Stork. At the subsequent inquiry Mr Krampf (Kemp) saw another side to his daughter. 'Old Krampf winced when he saw his daughter give a histrionic toss of her head in his direction. She was wielding the committee into a predatory pack who would chase anybody she pointed to.' Toply (Solicitor-General Burbury) 'thanked his lucky stars he had never been in her sights ... he knew nothing of young women who have a lifelong, sullen resentment toward their fathers.' Hilda was 'about as safe as a machine gun mounted on a merry-go-round'. Diaries and letters are forged, jewellery bought, drugs given and blackmail threatened. What is quite clear is that Panzee, 'Old Donald' as he labels the indefatigable amateur detective modelled on himself, believes this is what happened to Orr.[123]

He was predisposed to find conspiracies in the actions of people he didn't like, but Panzee also believed this because Orr had given him, and the Scots Kirk, a persuasive reason to believe it. This piece of 'new evidence', more than statements from distant students and companions in struggle, was what swung people in Orr's favour, although it was never stated in public. It was contained in a brief statement from Orr, dated 9 January 1958, in which he claims Suzanne told him in November 1955 that she was being subjected to sexual advances from her father.

He goes on: 'Regarding it as a fantasy at the time, I advised her to talk over her problems with a psychiatrist—Dr Engisch of Launceston—whom I notified by telephone about the matter. But she did not follow my advice. Dr Engisch is prepared to give evidence accordingly.'[124] (In fact, Dr Engisch was only prepared to say he had first met Orr after his dismissal and that they discussed the Orford letter. Only in 1964, by which time Orr was looking for evidence for another legal challenge, was Engisch prepared to say that Orr had communicated this information to him—after his dismissal.) For Panzee, who believed Orr to be utterly truthful, this information was dynamite. It was he who wrote to Hodgman on 18 January that 'It seems likely that Miss Kemp and Mr Kemp behaved as they did because Mr A [Allison] had obtained evidence of what Orr had communicated to Engisch. The blackmail power of such information would be enormous and fits in with textbook descriptions of behaviour in such relationships. Mr A's interest in the matter would be explained if he were acting as the agent of the VC's.'[125] Panzee had a keen eye for blackmail potential.

Hector Dunn, moderator of the Kirk, received an anonymous letter postmarked Sydney GPO, on 13 May, which hinted at aberrant behaviour between Suzanne and her father, and finished: 'this may be of some use in placing a new light on the professor's case.' Dunn was very concerned to find out who might have written this letter. Orr suggested it was one of Suzanne's girlfriends. The language however is pompous and masculine: 'I think it would pay dividends if the young lady in the case were questioned whether her father behaves in an unpaternal manner toward her—and whether his attitude is connived at.[126] It also has been typed on a typewriter which consistently gives the same uneven impression as the typewriter of one of Orr's very vocal supporters, a man with a fondness for pompous sentences. In their attempts to find out who might have penned this poisoned missive, the content of the letter was given to key Sydney journalists. Eddy too was well aware of Orr's evidence, since he described Suzanne as 'complicated in her emotional relationships with her father'. Even before Eddy's book hit the press a play written by Lance Peters, with a plot very similar to the Orr case (now being made into a film), had a brief run in Sydney. This play suggested an incestuous relationship between father and daughter.

Panzee spent years trying to get corroboration of this 'new evidence', which was reactivated every time a legal case was on the horizon. He got very little to show for his sleuthing, except that in 1965, when he was preparing for a lawsuit against the university, one of Orr's local enthusiasts, a journalist named John Hayes, reported that he had spoken to another journalist in Sydney who claimed to have seen father caress daughter through the window of the flat opposite his, in McLeay Street, in 1957. The journalist believed these people to be the Kemps because they were staying in Sydney at that time and he had recognised them from newspaper photos. In September 1965 Panzee rushed up to Sydney to interview this journalist and sent a report immediately to Orr's lawyer. The next day Panzee received a telegram from his source saying: 'Game irrevocably cancelled.'[127] Nothing further came to light; yet every person I have interviewed who was close to Orr and his supporters has told me this 'new evidence' was the 'real reason' for Orr's being set up. On two occasions I was told that Suzanne was a 'textbook case'. Each time the embellishments have been different: an academic from Tasmania had seen them in McLeay Street; a businessman from Hobart on a dirty weekend had the flat next door; and other variations. It is a piece of subterranean 'knowledge' that still flourishes.

I have pursued this evidence with the diligence of Panzee Wright and I believe it to be a total fabrication, even though it is quite possible that by two years after his dismissal Orr may have convinced himself that it was true, since the story is always sourced back to him. There was actually a tenuous connection between reality and the allegations, revealed in Reginald

Kemp's evidence to the university inquiry. Kemp told the inquiry that Orr apparently was very curious about Suzanne's relationship with her father, as the role of fathers intrigued him. During discussions she had told him that her father was 'not very affectionate' toward her, although every night he did come into her room to kiss her goodnight. To someone as obsessed with sex as Orr appears to have been, such actions could be converted into aberrant behaviour. In the heat of the moment, having been attacked by the outraged Reg Kemp, Orr tried to turn the tables by accusing Kemp of sexual impropriety toward Suzanne.

Significantly, Orr himself makes no reference to it in any court case, even though both Allison and Kemp repeated Orr's accusation at the university inquiry and the Supreme Court. The allegation would have been known to the High Court. It is interesting too that Hodgman said that during the Supreme Court case he was quite unaware of this possible explanation for Suzanne's behaviour, and that he heard of it later. In every case where I have been alerted to this 'evidence' I have found that the information trail leads directly back to Orr, sometimes via legal advisors, usually via mainland journalists, close to Orr. Invariably, the story I am told is that Orr had reluctantly, and in utmost confidence, given information on Suzanne's confessions about her father's behaviour, always insisting that he would never have allowed this material to be used in court. His selflessness and sense of honour is usually remarked upon.

One thing that seems very clear about Orr is his capacity to convince himself, and sometimes others, of his own delusions. It is conceivable that after six years of persistence Orr may even have convinced Dr Engisch that he had, in fact, spoken to him about Suzanne's neurotic behaviour. As for the story of a Sydney journalist gossiping about some activity he alleges he saw nine years earlier, I have been told by several journalists that Orr had confidentially put a story about Suzanne and her father into circulation when he made contact with them at a journalists' conference in Hobart during November 1957.

It is revealing that an intelligent male academic such as Panzee Wright was prepared to accept, on dubious evidence, that a wealthy businessman, whose family lived in Tasmania for generations, had molested his neurotic and promiscuous daughter and then coerced her into giving false evidence; than to accept, with compelling evidence, that an unstable professor known to have had an adulterous affair with a young woman had seduced an impressionable and naive student. Misogyny? Yes, there was undoubtedly some of that, his letters are full of unconscious denigration of women. But there was something else at work. Perhaps Orr's tale about Suzanne met certain expectations in the intellectual who had struck out for less parochial territory. Peter Conrad, another clever Tasmanian who escaped the narrow confines of his home state, filled pages of his book, *Down Home: Tasmania Revisited*, with jokes and asides about inbreeding and incest. For example: A young man from Ouse announced he had found a prospective wife who could read and write, and better, she was a virgin. 'No way,' said his father, 'If she is not good enough for her own family she is not good enough for us.' Did Panzee tell jokes like this too? Was this part of what made this spurious 'new evidence' seem to him like a 'textbook description'. For a man needing a plausible explanation for Suzanne's actions this one was tailor-made.

In 1958 only a very select group—journalists, lawyers and key Orr supporters—were aware of Orr's particularly sensitive 'new evidence'. I am fairly certain that the sympathetic churchmen, Bishop Cranswick and Archbishop Guildford Young, were told of it, as well as Moderator Dunn, but the confidence almost certainly did not extend to the 'naive' professors Stout and Montrose, who were so important in garnering support for Orr around the academic world. These idealists did not understand the aphorism about making omelettes. In private Panzee remarked to Eddy:

> I have the highest regard for Stout's integrity but less for his appreciation of the realities in society and even less for what to do ... He reminds me of a big shaggy dog, who will chase a stick for you into the water, come back showing appreciation of his own bravery and when you say 'good dog', he shakes himself and showers your new suit with pond water.[128]

The problem was that the philosophers saw the Orr case as a matter of abstract principle: Orr had been denied natural justice and a fair hearing. They did not want to get into the whys and wherefores of Orr's alleged sexual activity. The American advocate for Orr, Professor Glen Morrow, allowed that 'the undisputed facts of Orr's history were not very savoury,' but he would defend Orr 'because of the principles which seem to be violated in this case.' As well, he had great admiration for Stout and his colleagues 'for the stubborn fight you have made; I only wish our plaintiff had cleaner hands.'[129] Orr, with his volatile personality and his indiscretions, including the extraordinary six-part personal exposé in *Pix* in 1957, made heavy weather for the philosophers and their adherence to principle. As one Orr supporter wrote to Stout, 'It must leave one with the feeling that he has an almost infinite capacity for self deception and the University of Tasmania can no doubt argue that a man with so confused a mind is hardly likely to be a successful professor.'[130] Stout himself had little time for Orr as a philosopher and did not automatically expect him to be reinstated in his chair. As he pointed out to the University of Tasmania, his concern was that Orr got a proper hearing, not that they be forced to take him back: 'You would never have had him in the first place if you had taken the best advice—including mine!'[131] He was inclined to share the view of another Sydney colleague: 'Syd is after all a philosophical no-hoper'.[132] Stout's private hope was 'that *if* Orr is rehabilitated he may accept financial compensation and retraction of the allegation and yet not remain in the chair.'[133]

However, the steady stream of selected information about 'new evidence' seeping into Stout's publications began to muddy the waters of abstract principles, and increasingly issues of Orr's innocence came to the forefront. I have no doubt that the selected information Stout was being fed influenced his decision to push for a boycott on filling Orr's chair in 1958. To this course he persuaded the Australian Association of Philosophers as well as the philosophy associations overseas. He took it upon himself to write to prospective applicants for the chair and explain the lie of the land. To JP Day he stressed that there was new evidence that the University of Tasmania had refused to deal with, while 'rigorous analysis' by the Presbyterian Church had found the case against Orr not proven. 'I don't think the new professor's place in the community of philosophers would be a happy one' was his advice. He urged Day to show his letter to any other applicants, admitting 'all of this is highly irregular. But the whole business is extraordinary,' adding, 'I haven't passed on any of the persistent rumours about hidden motives, involving important political and business personalities in that strange community which help to make the fabrication suspicion plausible because you might think I was recounting the plot of a Ruritanian melodrama.'[134] Day withdrew his application, as did all other British applicants.

From Oxford Stout's son wrote to say that the boycott letter, published in the *Times* in June 1958, 'speaks so plainly that there is little danger of *anyone* over here reading it and yet applying.'[135] Stephen Toulmin at Oxford also contributed with a letter to colleagues 'couched in unexceptional terms so even those who dislike and distrust Orr will feel they ought to pass the message around ... damn it, I dislike Syd too, but the thing is too flagrant.'[136] In Oxford philosophers held strong opinions about Tasmania, with the eminent Gilbert Ryle referring to it as 'that loony bin'.[137]

Writing to an applicant in the United States, Stout made much the same case, with the same result. In all cases he stressed that the move was temporary and the chair would be open again since he confidently expected Orr would leave and go elsewhere. 'Above all,' he said, 'the philosophers want to see someone really good appointed to the chair.'[138] At home Stout's boycott got the support of almost all of the philosophical community during June 1958. In Melbourne, Boyce Gibson thought it utterly misguided, but in Sydney, David Armstrong, who thought Orr most likely guilty, agreed to support it. Jack Smart from Adelaide and Perc Partridge from the Australian National University were external members of the selection committee: in private they supported the boycott and had agreed not to make an appointment.

In discussion of the rights and wrongs of Orr's dismissal the issue of new evidence was much touted, along with the Scots Kirk finding. Although, Boyce Gibson pointed out, any intelligent person might ask 'Why should justice be better served by a church court which has watched only one face than a trained judge who has watched not only that face but all other relevant faces?'[139] Reliance on this 'new evidence' was severely shaken by the publication in August 1958 of a well-argued examination of the evidence by Hal Wootten and John Kerr in *Free Spirit*, mouthpiece of ACCF. It was a devastating piece and it blew the case of Orr and Panzee Wright right out of the water. Across Australia, philosophers began to get uneasy, especially those two external members of the selection committee. 'We all know Syd is a fool,' exploded Jack Smart, 'but anyone who assumed that he had a minimum of commonsense one is wont to associate with a professor would surely have taken his behaviour [in not co-operating with the inquiry] as a presumption of guilt.'[140] Partridge was especially nervous, writing to Stout: 'it seems to me that Panzee has taken a frightful thrashing and many of the allegations to which he gave currency have been shown to be half truths at the very best.' He felt it was 'desirable for someone to explain what exactly is the nature of the miscarriage of justice that calls for redress'.[141]

CHAPTER SEVEN

All the world knows my enemies

Wootten and Kerr may have dealt a body blow to Orr with their carefully argued piece 'Re-opening the Orr Case', but they were howled down by a torrent of denunciation and rebuttal from Panzee, and some others. Expecting the 'rough and tumble of debate' which would go with any controversial subject, Kerr and Wootten admitted they were surprised by 'the labyrinthine tortuosities, the obfuscation and plain misstatements with which untenable positions have been defended', not to mention 'the whispering campaign by which it was sought to smear us'.[142] Donald Horne, then editor of the *Observer*, frankly admits that his role at that time was to provide a forum for attacking Kerr and Wootten. Their names became synonymous with crafty double dealing in the Orrite lexicon. Many years later, Panzee, finding himself the object of attack by Orr, accused him of 'doing a Kerr Wootten on me'.[143]

After an initial attempt to answer almost unintelligible attacks on them, Wootten and Kerr threw in the towel. They were lawyers, each involved with complex legal battles quite separate from the Orr case, and they simply did not have the time for a protracted slanging match. Wootten was taken aback by the ferocity and scurrilous nature of the attack, but 'to keep up with it would have been a life's work ... I would have had to get down in the gutter and wrestle with all and sundry for years'.[144]

Faced with a no-contest, Panzee was able to drive home that these suspect lawyers had not been aware of the 'new evidence'. Stout reinforced this position, privately telling the dubious Partridge that 'theirs is a lawyer's opinion on old evidence.' New evidence, he confidently claimed, had been accepted by the Presbyterian church, and the Catholic Archbishop.[145] Along with a considerable number of thoughtful academics, Partridge remained unconvinced, but he need not have worried since there were no applicants for the chair of philosophy and he was no longer required for the selection committee. By September 1958 an international boycott of philosophers was in place.

Staff associations across the country were also talking of total boycotts, led by Newcastle University, which called for a black ban in July that year. Regular articles attacking the university in the Australian press, as well as articles in the *Times* in England, did considerable damage to the process of recruitment. The pressure on the university was becoming intolerable. Ken Buckley, secretary of FCUSA wrote to the staff association in Tasmania to implore it to cease supporting the administration's refusal to initiate a new inquiry:

> I am not sure that the members of staff realize how much damage has been done ... quite frankly I think whether or not there is a boycott, nobody of good quality in Australia or the UK will apply [for any academic positions] unless there has been a rehearing and justice has been seen to be done; to put it brutally, I think if the University Council maintains its present attitude the university might as well close down.[146]

In August 1958 the university entered the lists with a booklet written by its new vice-chancellor, Professor Keith Isles, who had returned to his home state after a distinguished career at Orr's alma mater in Belfast. Isles' decision to take the post was in no small way influenced by his indignation that his own university was under siege. Isles already had close personal contacts with several protagonists in the Orr battle. He had been one of a small group of intellectuals who formed a legendary wartime intelligence unit under Alf Conlon. Others included

Panzee Wright and John Kerr. Conlon, who had carried his wartime aura into backroom political influence in NSW, was an Orr enthusiast, and he had already made it his business to woo Isles to the cause. It was John Kerr, with whom Conlon had had an acrimonious parting of the ways, who persuaded Isles that the pro-Orr case was just huff and puff. However, Isles also formed the opinion that the council position on summary dismissal was unreasonable. He arrived to find an embattled and defensive council which had closed ranks against any talk of reason or compromise. While he favoured some kind of compromise whereby Orr might be given some financial assistance to quit the state, he was dragooned into writing a defiant public defence to be sent to universities around the world. At his elbow, supplying inflammatory drafts, were the chancellor, HS Baker, and legal advisor Reg Wright, whose stance Isles found uncomfortably combative.

In his booklet, published in late 1958, Isles pointed out in measured language the inappropriateness of the pro-Orr forces in demanding that the decision of two courts be disregarded and Orr reinstated. 'The spectacle of a university professor being ignominiously dismissed from his post is thoroughly distressing,' Isles wrote, but he had no patience with the suggestion that tenure was absolute, regardless of behaviour. 'High privilege demands, as its counterpart, a high degree of responsibility.' In the case of Orr, there could be 'no doubt that his conduct fell lamentably below the standards which a university can reasonably expect of its members and which academics can reasonably expect of each other'. It was regrettable that in his case the matter had had to go to court, however 'the desire of Australian academics to safeguard the security of academic tenure against any distasteful implication of the Court judgment will be frustrated if they persist in identifying it with the personal issues involved in the Orr case.'[147] These were sensible words, but they were given little heed. In fact, this booklet, which included both court judgements and was circulated to every university in

Australia and the UK, brought down on the unsuspecting Isles a defamation writ from Orr, which he took out in every state and country where the booklet had been distributed. Each writ specified damages of £50 000.

Orr was determined to get back into court, but he needed to do it in such a way that he could impugn the evidence of Suzanne Kemp. A critical point in his defence was that in the civil case, the requirement of proof were not those 'beyond all reasonable doubt'. It was her word against his own, he maintained, and given a higher proof or a different onus of proof, her story would not hold legal water. His luck improved when Suzanne arrived back in Australia on 18 September 1958. She was met at Sydney airport by her brother Andrew, who tried his best to shelter her from the intrusions of journalists and cameramen waiting for her arrival. In the Sydney *Sun*, beside a photo of her waiting by the luggage carousel is her sole comment: 'I want to forget the whole thing.'

Suzanne Kemp married Geoffrey Allison in Hobart less than a month later. Four days before her wedding, Orr was handing out thousands of roneoed statements to passers-by in the city centre. This clumsy document entitled 'A Challenge to Suzanne Kemp' was a direct invitation to issue a writ. 'I am reluctantly compelled to state ...' the large type ran. There followed a list of libellous allegations about falsifying evidence, lying under oath and defrauding the court. Suzanne was challenged 'as much for her own sake as mine' to take action, as these allegations could be tested. With other matters on her mind, the new Mrs Allison declined to rise to the bait, and subject herself to another court case. Proof in itself, claimed Orr and his loyal band of supporters, that she was the liar he said she was.

By this time Edwin Tanner had been forced to leave the state after being subjected to similar, if less flamboyant, pressure. As Tanner tells it, Orr repeatedly threatened to shoot him and his wife. In Melbourne he found himself 'being made to *feel guilty* by press and academic freedom fighters from as far away as

Scandinavia and the UK' in a process of vilification which lasted for ten years and in which he felt utterly helpless to defend himself.[148] He told his close friend Gwen Harwood that he had nightmares about being pursued by Orr supporters and was going to change his name: 'God himself knows what I've been through over telling on a philosopher. Edwin Iscariot. How's That?'[149]

Dr Milanov, left to carry the philosophy department alone, found himself the object of ridicule and abuse from students who had sat at Orr's knee and on the one occasion he ventured to the Philosophy Conference he was smartly made to understand he was persona non grata. When Ken Dallas returned from his sabbatical in 1957 he was upset to find that Orr had poisoned his colleagues' view of Milanov. Several philosophers I have spoken to, regardless of their sympathies with Orr, have seemed to regard Milanov as an intellectual nobody—not to be taken seriously as a philosopher. His appointment to a senior lecturer position in 1958 was widely deplored at the time. Yet Dr John Coleman found him an inspiring lecturer and another ex-student, Peter Cranswick, QC, remembers him as 'a marvellous man and a very good teacher'.[150] Certainly Milanov was not in the mainstream of Anglo-American philosophy at the time, being interested in European metaphysics. Most of his philosophical work had either been destroyed or remained, untranslated, in his native Serbian, but he was a scholar of some weight. Now that Serbian-speaking scholars are beginning to infiltrate the ranks of academe in Australia, it has become known that Milanov is very highly regarded in Yugoslavia, and that one of his books, *The Main Problems of the Theory of Knowledge*, is a standard text in that country. It is also clear that he was the victim of a communist purge in 1947, being dismissed from his university post and forced to flee the country.[151]

Panzee was not to be persuaded that Orr had treated Milanov badly and had violated his intellectual integrity. He wrote to Buckley, who had expressed concern on that point, saying:

'Actually having had some experience of continentals in my own department ... they can be the very devil when it comes to getting them to carry on ... in the co-operative way we expect from our own people.'[152] To Eddy he elaborated: 'those of us who have had NA's [New Australians] in our own departments know with what assiduity they try to dob in their seniors and their juniors.'[153]

Eddy, in discussing Milanov, is openly contemptuous, noting, significantly, that Milanov got his PhD in Berlin in 1933 and that it was conferred nine months after the Nazis came to power. Going through his war record with a fine-tooth comb, Eddy implies that Milanov had not been a professor in the department of philosophy and psychology at Belgrade in 1945–46, and is equally sceptical about Milanov's claims to major, but now destroyed, publications on Kant. His failure to secure a university position when he came to Australia, Eddy suggests, was because Milanov had problems with security, although Ken Dallas had investigated this rumour to the highest level and had received assurances from the solicitor-general that there were no security concerns about Milanov. (A fascinating connection is that Dallas, concerned that Milanov was being victimised on the basis of unsubstantiated rumours, had written to the Council of Civil Liberties for help in ascertaining Milanov's status. His letter was sympathetically received and passed on to the vigilant vice-president—Panzee Wright.) Moreover, the rumour that Milanov had been accused of being a communist, had been drawn to Dallas' attention by John Polya. Information once regarded as an attack on the civil rights of an immigrant thus became the basis for a virulent attack on his credibility. Both Milanov and the vice-chancellor, Hytten, are seen to share common ground, other than their European backgrounds—neither had 'fared well in free and open encounter with Professor Orr. They succeeded much better acting behind the scenes in their own quiet way ... men like Hytten and Milanov knew the requirements of tyranny with extraordinary intimacy.' Gratuitous? I thought so.

I was totally unprepared for the revelation that timid, terrified Dr Milanov was believed to be the puppet master in the conspiracy to frame Orr, or that he could be cast as an utterly sinister figure with shadowy connections to alien, authoritarian regimes that sought to undermine democracy in this country. When I first encountered references to Milanov as a Nazi in Panzee's notes, I could not quite take it in. Perhaps some bizarre, ironic aside I thought, remembering the number from Auschwitz tattooed on the arm of Mrs Milanov, her family's sole survivor from the holocaust—everyone who knew the Milanovs mentioned that tattoo; in Hobart in 1950 no one had ever seen such a thing before—and knew too the story of how Milanov had escaped from his Nazi captors by jumping from rolling stock; how he had collapsed in the snow and an older man had run past him and goaded him to his feet and to keep going.

But Panzee believed Milanov was a Nazi, or had been one. In 1957 Orr wrote to him suggesting that he check Milanov's past with the Yugoslavian Council 'which could give confirmation of Nazi collaboration and what happened in the war trials in Holland'.[154] War trials? What was this, I puzzled. Days of research later I unearthed another document in Panzee's voluminous archives. This was Orr's account of a conversation with a drunken Irishman (a schoolteacher) in a pub in Hobart on 9 May 1959. It is written up as a confidential note, very important.

> In the course of the conversation it appeared that Burke (an Irishman, or of Irish descent and Catholic) was originally in N.S.W., more than usually educated and ... appeared to have been in or connected with the armed forces during the war and to have some association with Security or Security Officials, and informed me at one stage (in response to my probing) that the man I should get in touch with was Black

Jack Callaghan. He appeared to have been drinking for some time, and by the time the following remarks were elicited he was well under the weather.

My interest was aroused by his confident assertion at one stage that Milanov was the *real* cause of my trouble. On being questioned carefully he gave the following information: He had known him in Dachau Camp as a Nazi indoctrinator and psychological aide of some sort. He described most graphically—using M's characteristic mannerisms—how contemptuously Milanov used to treat the prisoners, always ending up with (in German) 'THAT IS *THE* PHILOSOP*HEE*!' He suggested that he himself had been psychologically 'treated' by Milanov, who caused a 'blockage' in his mind (NOTE M USED THIS VERY TERM IN HIS TALKS WITH ME and claimed he could do such a thing and had been successful in 'cases' in the past, e.g. he broke a 'fixation' between a man and a woman by means of a 'loaded' letter he got the former to write, which 'struck the right chords with the unconscious' of the recipient! hence his insistence that I write such a letter to A!). Burke claimed that this 'blockage' still prevents him from remembering 'something important' which apparently M determined he should forget; and he behaved like a man struggling to recall something and distressed because he couldn't. Most significant was the fact that he used phrases peculiar to M's psychological jargon, imitated his way of going on and his Nazi-like dogmatism and ruthlessness, to such a degree of perfection that would seem to be impossible unless he had had close personal experience of M.

He 'let out' (in answer to my line 'What the devil is Security in this country doing anyway that it isn't on to all that went on in Orr case, etc') that Security was watching M but had been letting him run on a long

> leash because they suspected he was the leader of a Nazi organisation in this country (Note: this accords with the kind of thing the Secretary of Civil Rights Council in Melb. told me after H.C. when they gave me a booklet on Psycho-politics) but that they were going to move in on him in about 3 months time? They were well aware of what he had been up to in the Orr case, etc. To my persistent request to be put in touch with Security he gave me first the above name of the top man; and later the name of someone in the T & G Buildings Collins Street, whom he said I could approach.
>
> He also said something about having been connected with the War Crimes tribunal at Nuremberg, and having seen Milanov there—apparently on trial or about to be tried (but by this time he had had too much to drink to get clarity from him).[155]

Now, I know that some Yugoslavians were Nazi collaborators during the war, although they tended to be Croatian not Serbian, just as I am aware that some fathers molest their daughters. But it was beginning to look like the Orr defence was spinning into the realms of malicious absurdity. As my research expanded I found myself increasingly probing the intricacies of a full-blown international conspiracy with very unpleasant overtones.

The idea seems to have come first from Orr, by way of Eric Butler of the Victorian League of Rights, a neo-Nazi organisation. Butler had contacted Orr following his High Court defeat and given him a book on psycho-politics featuring analysis of the Moscow show trials. Orr was quick to see the acute similarities between these trials and what had happened to him. The techniques used were the same; no doubt they had been learnt from the same people. Eddy, who had also been making a study of communist mind-control techniques, agreed. He followed up with the Victorian League of Rights, receiving further pamphlets and communications from Butler. He could see that this xenophobic and anti-Semitic organisation tended to ratbaggery, 'but they can see some things missed by the respectable ... and psycho politics is, in substance, genuine. It is simply a systematic statement of what I have observed myself, except until I had read it I had not linked the mental therapy business with it.'[156] Did this mean that they were up against 'a bunch of coms' he wondered to Panzee and Orr. None of them had any doubts that they were dealing with a sophisticated conspiracy in which the Kemps were mere pawns. But who was behind it?

Eddy had already built his book on Orr around the premise of a conspiracy. Donald Horne, still firmly in the Orr camp, had seen an early draft in December 1958 and was simply amazed at the lunatic bent of it. His magazine, the *Observer*, had been intending to publish the book. He and a mutual friend had lunch with Eddy and were treated to a rave about a conspiracy directed from eastern Europe, so secret that not even the KGB knew about it. Horne contacted Alan Stout about this turn of events in considerable alarm.[157]

Stout's reaction was to telephone Eddy and quiz him on his intentions. Eddy described this interrogation in a bitter letter to Panzee and Orr. He was worried that Stout would veto the book unless he could be converted. Stout had 'queer ambivalences', Eddy thought, especially as he had said 'Panzee is mad' when told that Panzee believed the conspiracy to be orchestrated from within the United States, probably by the CIA.[158] Panzee did not care to be called mad. He defended his position by pointing out that American interests believed Australia was the last white country with skilled people and that the union structure could be undermined here. It was no accident that Grouper tactics had targeted unions, especially in the Hursey case on the Hobart waterfront. Kerr and Wootten, members of ACCF, had both been involved in the Hursey case and the ACCF had links with the CIA. Stout himself, Panzee was quick to point out, was a member of the ACCF, although 'how anyone could remain so without dying of hyperemesis defeats me.'[159]

It was Eddy's thesis about forces from behind the Iron Curtain which proved more persuasive. Panzee told Stout that Eddy made him feel humble because 'his capacity as a social scientist to see the associations and interrelations leave me convinced and gasping'.[160] In time the CIA connection dropped out of view as the trio sifted through the evidence to identify the main conspirators. Hytten, the New Australian vice-chancellor was an obvious target, and Panzee detailed one of his journalist mates in England to see what could be dug up about his past. 'A biography of Hytten may be the key to the full solution and certain victory,' Eddy thought. Absolute secrecy must be maintained. 'I'm sorry to sound cloak and dagger, but I'm serious ... I'm not playing a blind hunch here.'[161] The obvious others were Allison, Chief Justice Burbury and, perhaps, Townsley. And what about Townsley's friend in the economics department, Ken Dallas? He was a communist, wasn't he? Panzee had noted 'he had a thing about N A's' and had been a major support for Milanov.[162] Even Ken Buckley, as another left-wing economist and possible fellow traveller became suspect, since in Panzee's view his interventions in the case only created more trouble. 'Dallas had been extraordinarily active anti-Orr,' Eddy reported,[163] and Dallas was a mate of Buckley's.

While all this speculation was going on, they would have been fascinated to know that Frank Knopfelmacher, a vehement anti-communist crusader, whom they loathed, believed the communists to be manipulating *them*! In a letter to ACCF he drew attention to the 'sinister character' of the Orr defence, saying: 'You don't build up a stunt of these dimensions just like that and [the Orr camp] has taken in astute and wily people such as some of the Catholics. It seems one cannot be suspicious enough of these characters such as Wright ...'[164] Ken Dallas, on the other hand, was suspicious that security forces were funding the pro-Orr case in order to keep the chair of philosophy vacant, thus excluding any left-wing influence in this strategic academic field, just as, he believed, they had influenced the rejection of the much admired historian and communist, George Rudé.

By 1959 the trio of investigators had their attention focused fully on Milanov: 'All along there have been signs of a grey eminence,' wrote Eddy, 'but it has been hard to pin him down.' All three were quite convinced that 'psychopolitics is at the heart of this case' and so the finger pointed directly to 'Milanov the not-so-ex-Nazi who learned the tricks of the psycho political trade' during the war. But was it just Milanov on his own or 'was he aided and abetted by the coms, or is he their own? That is the crux.' As Eddy developed this theory, both the chief justice and the vice-chancellor became integral to the plot. It was possible that all three 'were coms undercover' and had 'learnt the techniques of the party line', especially Chief Justice Burbury: 'the resemblance struck me forcefully', Eddy remarked, straightfaced.[165]

One thing was sure: 'the Supreme Court judge had to be a com.—or whoever wrote the Judgment.' No judge in the history of British law could write a judgement like that unless he were a member of some covert organisation, Eddy insisted. 'If Green wrote the Judgment then he is the centre ... it is a meticulous piece of work written to deceive the High Court in particular by someone who understood perfectly what was being done to Orr and who used the same techniques in the judgment at every point.'[166] But all three were disinclined to think Green wrote this judgement, despite the possibility of his being blackmailed into it. Only one man was in a position to stand over Green; 'that one was Burbury.' Paul Berry had analysed the Green judgement and found signs of the chief justice's style in it. Burbury, along with Hytten, must have been recruited by Milanov, unless of course, Burbury himself was the centre, and that was a real possibility.

Am I stretching your credibility here? Surely these people

are just playing looney tunes to amuse themselves you think? I am afraid not. In Orr, Panzee and Eddy were a curious combination of paranoid personalities, albeit each with a different slant. Each was able to feed the conspiratorial fantasy of the other, so the cumulative effect was an escalating paranoia, greater than the sum of its parts. They wrote to each other in a kind of conspiratorial shorthand so each could fill in the missing detail according to his own particular bent. To Orr the conspiratorial 'they' meant anyone who opposed his will, whereas Eddy and Panzee needed to force the cabal of Orr's accusers and opponents into some political configuration which found echoes in the wider society. In this way they were able to give their obsession with Orr real credibility and transcend his only-too-obvious shortcomings as a person. Orr was happy to go along with any theory which absolved him and placed him at the centre. The paranoid fallacy is integral to the public defence of Orr and while the most bizarre accusations of conspiratorial intrigue are confined to the trio's letters, in essence the conspiracy theory as developed underpins the opus which Eddy was writing, with help from Panzee and Orr.

It is Milanov who clearly emerges as the villain of the book. As Eddy explained to the sceptical Stout, there was no denying that 'Milanov manifests most skilfully the pattern of attack.'[167] Milanov had made the first complaint against Orr. He had previously secured Orr's trust, and to a degree dependence, by psychoanalysing him, which gave Milanov the opportunity to use his mind-control techniques. Milanov also was aware of the contents of A's letter, which was used in court and, most telling, had given the university documentation of Orr's dreams. These sensitive documents had been the basis of cross-examination, but what most interested Eddy was the similarities between evidence against Orr and things to be found in his dreams and in A's letter. Evidence had been carefully manufactured by someone familiar with that letter and the dreams, and there was no mistaking who that person might be.

In his book Eddy invites the reader to conclude that a 'secret document' must have been the basis for the 'fictitious character attributed to [Orr] by his enemies'. The similarity between the letter from A and Suzanne's supposed diary was unmistakable. 'Careful study of the evidence of each of the accusers suggests their painstaking character portrayals must be coming from a common source.' It was Panzee who suggested that the source was A's letter, only obliquely referred to in court. It was Orr, presumably, who supplied Eddy with a copy, after the original had been returned to A at her lawyer's insistence. Panzee makes certain observations about the letter and its author, based on what Orr had told him: 'A herself is a neurotic, introspective and given to the study of the mind and mental problems.' According to Panzee, the medical expert, her portrait of Orr was not to be taken seriously, since she had dished up to the bishop a 'textbook case' of schizophrenia drawn from her observations of people with this problem. Her own brother had been institutionalised, he confided.[168]

This 'secret document', itself the product of a disturbed mind, was used to tailor the evidence of university witnesses, Panzee was sure. That is why it was said that Orr had delusions of grandeur, that he importuned favours, that he was obsessed with sex; that he was violent and given to long harangues—each accusation part of the litany against Orr in A's letter. Witnesses even put the same phrases into Orr's mouth when describing his behaviour. Why, it was even claimed he said almost exactly the same thing to Suzanne that he said to A. Collusion. No doubt about it.

As letters went back and forth between Orr, Panzee and Eddy, speculation was continuous as to who else might be drawn into the conspiracy. Allison had been recruited by Milanov early, that was clear. And of course Poga, another eastern European, was in on it. What about that other New Australian, John Polya? It was true that in 1959 he was firmly back in the Orr camp but 'his actions in 1955 at several critical points were just what the attack needed,' Eddy insisted. Orr had got the measure of Milanov and Hytten after the royal commission, but he had continued to trust and confide in Polya. 'It is astounding how many of Polya's actions are capable of construction both ways.'[169] In his letters Orr was keen to point out what a fair-weather friend Polya had proved to be. Perhaps he also brought with him sinister intentions from his native Hungary. Poga, Hytten and Polya were all most likely being run by Milanov. More recently he had recruited the locals: Burbury, Allison, Townsley and others. But for what purpose?

Whatever did they believe Milanov hoped to get from all this clandestine activity? Two things, according to Panzee: 'to disrupt Australian institutions and to get a job for Milanov'.[170] A full appreciation of how profound Panzee thought the disruption of Australian institutions could be can be gained from reading his unpublished novel, The Cuckoo, written in 1960. In this book a democratic island state eventually disintegrates into a state of totalitarian dictatorship in a steady progress from the framing of a leading dissenter, through the destruction of the university, the undermining of unions, massive social unrest and, finally, totalitarian repression. All this is masterminded by Radek, a central figure who 'distils all the evils of totalitarianism' and is cunningly omniscient. On the surface, though, Radek is an apparently harmless and quiet central European who lectures in politics and dabbles in psychoanalysis.

The opening chapter of the novel, in which Old Donald is told by Paddy O'Rourke of Radek's 'diabolical' power, is an imaginatively expanded version of Orr's encounter with the well-lubricated Irishman. Panzee, it is clear, took this absolutely seriously. As the book progresses, the reader sees how Radek has planned the downfall of Professor Stork as the first step in destroying the democratic fabric of the community. In his armoury are mind control, hypnosis, drugs, forged documents and manufactured evidence, all dealt out unobtrusively behind the scenes. Of course he has help from a university run by immoral, ambitious men, who are 'natural liars who could speak with studied inexactitude or tell three different versions of the same incident in the most engaging way'. Likewise, he is abetted by the unsuspecting legal fraternity who 'did not realize Radek's part in the whole business and did not realize the depth of amorality and spinsterish spite of old academic hacks whose IQ was 140 but whose level of deception would shame a Neapolitan pimp'.

Panzee's novel was meant to 'carry on the story and show how psychopolitics works out', while Eddy's book was to demonstrate, using the observable facts 'how a social leadership can be got to discredit itself, betray its own standards, and produce a major social catastrophe'.[171] The victims, Eddy told Stout, were the High Court, the whole legal system, the press, the universities, the police—those just for a start. 'But of course I am not allowed to enter into any of this and if I did some people (most people, nearly all?) would say: this is crazy.'[172]

He did have to tone it down considerably for publication, and one whole chapter on conspiracy was excised, although the conspiratorial language and the explicit reference to Hytten and Milanov as malign foreign influences, remained. This much was essential because, Eddy explained to his publisher at Jacaranda Press, 'this is the first time these techniques of framing have been put on record in a democratic society.'[173] The in-house reader wrote:

> If Eddy is right, here is Moloch again in different form—the devourer of liberty and academic freedom—grinning awfully at us from across the Tasman Sea. Van Diemen's Land? Veritably a land of demons ... could there be still operating there some malign influence dating back to the bloodstained days of its early penal history? Fantastic? That's how it affected me.[174]

Just how many people were being treated to the conspiracy theory is hard to tell, thirty-five years later. It seems distinctly odd now, but the atmosphere was deeply unsettled in the 1950s and academics were genuinely worried that intellectual repression akin to McCarthyism would infect Australian life. It was a period of intense anxiety in the intellectual community about how much alien and clandestine processes were infiltrating Australia. These concerns were the staple of the ACCF which, at least as late as 1959, numbered amongst its members a great many leading liberal academics. In the libertarian left there was understandable concern about political interference from ASIO in the process of selection and appointment of staff. Ken Buckley himself had feared he would not get an academic position in Australia because of his radical left associations. He knew that ASIO had a file on him. It was generally believed that Russel Ward had been denied a lecturership in history at the University of New South Wales in 1960 because of direct political interference. The same was felt about the rejection of George Rudé at Tasmania, although he did get a job at Adelaide. Ken Dallas initially had a passport refused him by the Commonwealth, acting on ASIO advice, when he wanted to go to England on study leave in 1954. The incipient Democratic Labor Party, initially known as the Grouper movement, was very active in attempting to split left-wing unions with communist leadership from the Australian Labor Party and to break the power of these unions, most infamously in the Hursey case; and of course there was the Petrov affair to feed the fears of both left and right. In this context, what may seem today like rampant paranoia was common enough, and acceptable, in the late 1950s, with World War II not yet a distant memory and the hysteria of the Cold War rife. The country was filling up with different kinds of people who brought with them the traumas and ancient animosities of their homelands. But even in an environment where talk of conspiracy was commonplace and suspicion came readily, the theories developed in the tortuously long letters which ran between Orr in Hobart, Panzee in Melbourne and Eddy in Sydney along with those of the disreputable League of Rights, from whom they got their first clues about the conspiracy, were on the bizarre extreme. One wonders how academics would have been prepared to give Orr the time of day if they had realised the company he was prepared to run with, or the tactics he was prepared to use. I certainly hope that was the case, although given the number of academics who understood that Orr was a fool, and probably a liar, I could be disappointed.

Since paranoia engendered caution, the modus operandi of the three prime movers was to play their cards close to the chest. They would give out hints of impending legal reassessment to the second lieutenants like Stout and Buckley, who were continually fed tantalising, if not necessarily accurate, snippets of new evidence which promised a legal reversal—if only the bitter, mean-minded and recalcitrant university would allow a new inquiry. The job of these lieutenants was to keep chivvying along the academic associations to support Orr, now that he was apparently on the brink of a turnaround. Panzee also took on the role of peripatetic advocate, visiting campuses around the country, sometimes with Orr in tow, blitzing staff associations with minute details of the evidence of Orr's court case. In the absence of any alternative reading—most academics had been quite unaware of the case at the time—Panzee was able to mount a very persuasive case on Orr's behalf.

Many staff associations donated money to Orr. Panzee himself provided large amounts of direct financial support to the Orr family. Interestingly, at Sydney University, where academics were most vocal in their indignation against Orr's dismissal, there was real resistance to putting hands in academic pockets. Nevertheless Sydneyites, along with other staff associations, continued to dissuade their colleagues, in Australia and abroad, from applying to Tasmania. (Sandy Porteous was subject to this pressure when he was offered a job in the English department.

He found it very disquieting to get a number of unsolicited letters speaking so negatively of his prospective employer when he was at the other end of the world, in Edinburgh. He thought long and hard about whether to take the job and decided, ultimately, that the Tasmanian community had a right to a university. His decision was confirmed, he felt, when, soon after his arrival, he heard the president of FCUSA, Professor Thorpe of Sydney University, assert that the university should be brought to its knees.) Financial and moral support came from the Association of Philosophers, led by Stout, which continued its boycott against filling Orr's chair, despite disquiet about how long the chair was to remain vacant. It was agreed that students could not be indefinitely denied philosophic teaching (Milanov largely being disregarded) and distinguished visitors were permitted to act in Orr's position. These included Professor Fox from the University of Western Australia, and Orr's own supervisor, Professor Macbeath from Queen's, Belfast, who arrived in late 1959.

As Orr's supervisor and one of his referees, Macbeath looked a very likely ally in the Orr cause. With this in mind Stout wrote to him before he left Belfast to acquaint him with the developments in the case. He received an amiable, if disheartening, letter in return. 'I have no objection to discussing Orr's case with you,' wrote Macbeath.

> I have known him for many years and have had plenty of opportunities of forming my own opinion of him. There would seem to be many people in Australia who want to supply me with information about him if I may judge from the rather voluminous correspondence I have received. This correspondence is very like that which I received when he was in trouble in this country ...[175]

Correspondence between the two continued, although Macbeath remained tight-lipped about what that 'trouble' might have been, until he arrived in Tasmania and felt the full force of Panzee's scorn. He held off, he explained to Stout the following year, because 'I did not want to kick a man when he is down.'[176]

Orr, fearing some revelations from Macbeath, had warned Panzee that he had had differences with his old professor. Writing to Montrose in Belfast, Panzee wanted further information to help him deal with Macbeath. 'As my name is not Macduff I need assistance ... my aim is to put Macbeath off-side on first meeting.' As he understood it, the matter between Orr and Macbeath was 'at a purely intellectual, academic level ... intellectual conflict with personal disparagement being regarded as a normal academic incident in schools of philosophy.'[177] Orr told him that Macbeath had regarded his work on Plato as too radical. Montrose appears not to have answered, so Panzee was left with Orr's word. After Macbeath arrived in September 1959, Panzee set about disparaging the emeritus professor with his usual gusto.

With Vice-Chancellor Isles, whom he found under threat of multiple libel actions, Macbeath was not so reticent, informing his old friend of Orr's problems at St Andrews and how similar, if informal, allegations of improper conduct had been made during his short stay at that university. By late 1959 rumours of previous allegations against Orr began to surface on the mainland. Despite Panzee's barnstorming public-relations exercises, sceptical people began to ask just what was the nature of the 'new evidence'. To some it was beginning to sound suspiciously like a lot of hot air. If Orr had evidence, they wanted to know, why did he not use this to demand another court hearing? Others wondered why he did not apply for another job and get on with his life.

By this time he was insistent that without a retraction from the university he was unemployable. Among themselves many philosophers agreed that Orr was unemployable, but only because he was a bad philosopher. David Armstrong was especially forthright in his opinion of Orr as a 'no-hoper', and he was not alone, with even solid supporters like Stout decidedly unimpressed with Orr's academic potential.[178] However, there were jobs at a lower academic level which he could have got: he could have begun again, as he had after St Andrews, at a community college in Rapid Springs, Idaho, or somewhere like that.

But no, he stayed fixed in Hobart, keeping himself busy with re-examination of the evidence against him and surrounded by a small band of loyal supporters, every inch the martyr he had once foreshadowed. The student population was his most responsive recruiting ground, more likely because they wanted to cock a snoot at the administration than out of concern for the man himself. In 1959 he was elected honorary patron of the arts students club and the following year gave an address to freshers. *Togatus*, the student newspaper, gave Orr enthusiastic coverage, year in and year out. Tony Manley, a one-time editor, told how each year Orr 'would rush down to the *Togatus* cubby hole when the new editor moved in to get her/him onside'.[179] To any number of observers it looked as though Orr had found a comfortable niche and the limelight his mediocre scholarship would never have brought him. Very few appreciated his continued presence in the town. Rather tartly, Gwen Harwood reported that 'Sydney continues to live in his palace and waves like the Pope toward passers-by who look up at him.'[180]

From time to time Orr received a shot in the arm from across Bass Strait when the heavies flew in. Thorpe and Buckley came in late 1958 on behalf of FCUSA and published a report most ungenerous in its assessment of the university. In October Panzee came to stir up the local staff association and to get some evidence first-hand. He interviewed lots of people and filled his diary with scurrilous tittle-tattle about Suzanne Kemp's personal life. He was told by Geoff Harrison that he had warned Orr about playing around with Suzanne, but this evidence was disregarded in favour of gossip and innuendo. Clem Christensen, the editor of *Meanjin*, provided illustrious help in his detective work, accompanying Panzee to Bellerive beach to hold the other end of the tape measure while they measured the distance between road and culvert where Orr's car had got stuck. Christensen's presence in Tasmania was not lost on Gwen Harwood: 'I wonder if *Meanjin* is going to join the Swine's Chorus?' she mused to Tanner.[181]

Panzee's impassioned defence of Orr made some inroads among the staff in Hobart, but not the administration. With Macbeath's information, the vice-chancellor was encouraged in his determination to resist calls for a new inquiry, which he knew would be an expensive waste of time. Privately he was inclined to follow the advice of his long-term friend, John Kerr, and pay Orr the six months salary in lieu of notice to get rid of him. It gave him no pleasure to know that nearly four years after his dismissal, Orr was still on the university's doorstep, unemployed, burdened with legal costs, financially dependent on handouts and the meagre salary his wife earned as a cook and cleaner at the local kindergarten. But whatever his personal feelings about the Orr family trauma, Isles' public face was the unyielding position of the council that Orr would get nothing from the university.

Two days before Christmas 1959, at about 10 pm, when Orr was entertaining two student supporters, the phone rang and Orr went downstairs to a rarely-used office to take the call. When he switched on the light he was clearly visible through the uncurtained windows. As he answered the phone, someone fired a high-calibre rifle through the window, then sped off. Orr was wounded with a graze on his right temple and burns on the tips of his right-hand finger and thumb. His startled guests rang the police and several Melbourne newspapers. According to these newspapers, which published photos of Orr's grazed temple and his broken window, he had received a crude anonymous letter immediately after the shooting, warning that the next attempt would be fatal. That was duly photographed as well. On Boxing Day *Truth* emphasised Orr's denial that the shooting was a publicity stunt.

On 5 January, Harry Robertson, a well-known repossession agent, described as a wrestler and detective, was arrested. The police ballistics evidence said the rifle was his. Robertson had an alibi for his whereabouts, but even so he was concerned someone was trying to make a patsy out of him. According to the police, on the evening that Robertson was arrested he was permitted to make a telephone call. The call was to Paul Berry. By prearrangement Robertson and Berry agreed to a meeting. Detective Superintendent Fletcher listened to the conversation and formed the opinion 'the man Berry had some knowledge of the matter which he [Robertson] spoke about.'[182] On 30 January, The *Herald* reported Robertson as saying that he had been approached by Paul Berry offering help and legal aid and that Berry was purporting to be representing Orr. He alleged that Berry told him finance would be arranged by Orr supporters in Melbourne. 'I thought it was just a hoax,' Robertson said. 'Now it looks like I've been framed over it.' The police interviewed Berry but no charges were laid.

At the trial, evidence was given by the government pathologist who inspected the wound. He said: 'I don't know what caused the wound to Professor Orr's head.' He was surprised that the wound had not included the ear, as one would expect from a high-velocity object, and felt it could have been caused by Orr 'drawing some sharp object two or three times across that portion of his head.' He did not definitively rule out a ricochet from a portion of fragmented bullet. As to the white burns on the tip of Orr's finger and thumb, he 'had never seen a wound like that caused by a bullet in flight', but it 'could have been caused by picking up a bullet fragment when very hot'. Expert witness was given by Panzee, who had examined the wounds nearly three weeks later and felt them to have been caused by a bullet fragment which ricocheted from the windowsill. He also gave evidence that a bullet fragment is not solid above 200 degrees and could not cause a white burn on the fingers.[183] He had tested his theory about burns, he told the court, by holding his hand against a hotplate at 300 degrees. The case was dismissed because the magistrate felt the ballistic evidence was too slender to commit. He did say that he was satisfied the shooting was not a hoax, although a great many in Hobart thought otherwise, including one person who was in the Orr house that night.

Nation carried an unsigned but highly charged account of the shooting the following month, written, as it happens, by Panzee Wright. 'So the well propagated slanders on Orr rebounded,' the article concludes, allowing that on this occasion the debased legal system—but not the police—had done the right thing. 'Evidence showed that departments responsible for the administration of justice spent their energies on trying to inveigle Orr's friends into legal indiscretions while ... the assassins remain at large.' The piece ends with some characteristic flourishes. 'Incredible? Not if you know Hobart. Serious? Most serious—there are other Australian cities where it could happen ... The acceptance of assassination in a community means that every citizen is at the mercy of an enemy who can afford to pay the price.' Orr, it was apparent, was a serious threat to the interests of just such an enemy.

Orr himself immediately saw the parallels between Trotsky, whom the communists had tried to assassinate in 1940, and his experience. It was the same pattern of attack. The coms had tried to blame Trotsky for his own attempted assassination, saying it was a hoax, just as they had about Orr. Eddy was not entirely pleased with the embrace of Trotsky since he was, as far as Eddy could see, just as suspect as the coms ... he was a com of sorts, was he not? But Orr had decided that the mantle of Trotsky would suit him well. During Orientation Week he gave a talk to students in which he emphasised that Suzanne Kemp was 'as much a victim of this whole conspiracy' as himself. 'This girl has been more destroyed,' he ventured, 'because I can demonstrate my innocence. Can she?' Warming to the theory of conspiracy, he quoted Trotsky: 'All the world knows my enemies.' Students should not be complacent, he warned, 'it is not eastern Europe where this is happening. It is in Australia.'[184] Shortly after, he left Hobart for his own safety and went to live in Sydney at the home of his compatriot, Harry Eddy.

CHAPTER EIGHT

It may be true, but it is irrelevant

Apart from the pain of family separation, Orr found numerous advantages to being domiciled in Sydney. He was able to keep in close contact with FCUSA members to remind them of their duty toward him and he was able to keep an editorial eye on the book Eddy was still writing. With so many other of his supports pulled from under him, Orr felt that everything was riding on this book. He felt authorial responsibility as well, since much of his own work had gone into it. The book was nominally Eddy's, and Eddy was determined to keep it that way, yet both Orr and Panzee had contributed hugely to it with material from books they were in the process of writing. Orr had basically written the first four sections on the royal commission and university politics, as well as supplying voluminous material on the evidence and court cases. Eddy had sent working drafts of chapters, to which Orr had responded with extensive deletions and substitutions often running to twenty or thirty closely typed foolscap pages for each chapter. Panzee's responses were also substantial, if not so very detailed.

So as to recognise the relationship the three had in this project, and try to safeguard his own authorship, Eddy had drafted a contract between them as early as March 1959. This draft specified that Eddy 'must retain the right to publish or not publish' but that the author profits would be split between the three of them.[185] A formal contract, amended by Orr and Panzee, was drawn up by Orr's Sydney solicitor in August 1960. This deed specified that Eddy had written the book 'materially assisted by Orr and Wright' and that copyright was his but that royalties were to be divided between them. One year and several drafts later Eddy had still not signed, even though a stipulation of the agreement between the three was that Eddy could not sign a contract with Jacaranda Press until this contract had been finalised.

Brian Clouston, from Jacaranda, felt Eddy 'was a bit cheesed off about being pushed around, and not being consulted about this book (which is after all his)'.[186] Clouston sympathised, earning himself a sharp rebuke from Panzee: 'I prefer you did not give Harry advice re his relations with Syd and me. You probably do not realize how much of Harry's book is taken from manuscripts of Syd's and myself … without Syd in Sydney I doubt it would ever have been completed.'[187] Realising that it was Panzee with whom he should deal, not the putative author, Clouston agreed to send several copies of galleys to Panzee and to pay Orr an income of £10 a week as Eddy's assistant on the book as an advance against royalties.[188] That took care of all the royalties, since the business of correcting the manuscript (and rewriting the galleys) took nine months. It was understood that no one outside a close circle should know about the close collaboration between author and subject.

Throughout 1960, while living in Eddy's house, Orr was able to insist on substantial changes to the book. Eddy, while he fought for his own interpretation, always felt hamstrung by the fear that 'they' would assassinate Orr and frame him with it. If there were known to be tensions between them the framing would be a snap, he feared, especially with the infiltration of communists everywhere he turned. Holding out against Orr was a stressful business, and by November the tension was palpable. Orr wrote to Panzee that 'my position here has become well nigh untenable,' complaining about Eddy's suspicion about the book and his not having signed the contract. His lawyer had 'firmly pointed out' to Eddy that the agreement between the three of them must be completed before a contract with Jacaranda. He was adamant that 'This book is the Orr story, in more senses too than the fact that it contains our documents and had been produced with joint assistance the whole time by SSO and RDW.'[189] At the same time Eddy wrote to Stout that 'Syd was so keen on so much going in' and whatever Eddy took out, Orr would put back in again. Eddy allowed that the period of cutting (or not cutting) the book 'was a period of difficulty between Syd and me',[190] whereas Orr said bluntly 'one of these days I'll pack up and go.'[191] He did not say where he might go.

As well as strong views about the content, each of the trio had a preferred title. Orr wanted *A Philosopher Pilloried* whereas Panzee fancied *From Malice to Murder*. Eddy's preferred title was *Orr: A Case Study in Victimization*. They settled on *Orr*, which nobody much liked.

Writing to Stout in December, Eddy came clean with his worries, then crossed out the sensitive lines. They are clearly visible nonetheless. He wrote: 'I fear the control of the text is going completely out of my hands and so I let minor items go. I fear I may be confronted with a cut and revised book and given the option of rejection, with further delays and costs, or accepting what I don't want, or accepting joint authorship which would mean the book could only damage ...' Here he stops, realising he has already said too much.[192]

Orr returned to Hobart for Christmas, taking the galleys of the book with him. From that distance he had the advantage over a distraught Eddy who blew a fuse in January on discovering that Orr had written in highly damaging material. 'If this goes in,' he wrote to Orr 'I would be your stooge, because I am completely unconvinced ... if you push ruthlessly enough you come close to dictation.'[193] By May his worst fears were being realised. 'What I see in page proofs is very different to what I wrote and I thoroughly disapprove. I see this at the last minute when all must be finished by the weekend,' he remonstrated with Orr.[194] To Panzee he complained that Orr was dealing directly with the printer and deliberately bypassing him. 'I am entitled to see what the printer has put in as my text.' He would not accept that Orr should take responsibility for any errors, since it was supposed to be *his* book. It had his name on it and he would be the one sued. Already he could envisage the cross-examination when he would have to admit that Orr actually wrote that section.[195] The book was months overdue, horribly long and the publisher was getting furious, yet Orr kept insisting on more and more going in. Eddy knew Jacaranda was going to lose money and this he would have to wear even though it was not his fault. The revisions took six months and the book ran over 800 pages. In all it was an unhappy business. And he still had no contract with his publishers.

I was intrigued to see that a laudatory review of the book, written by historian Brian Fitzpatrick, appeared in the April issue of *Meanjin*, nearly a month before it was published—a rather unusual procedure. At the time of its publication Eddy was still trying to wrest revised page proofs from Orr. Not that Eddy was ignorant of the review. He had actually received a copy of it prior to publication for his comment—an even more unusual practice. In his response to the draft review, Eddy noted that the publisher would have some difficulty with the timing, but otherwise confined the content of his seven-page, single-spaced, foolscap letter to the changes he would like Fitzpatrick to make. Two pages concerned general points of interpretation, but the remaining five pages got down to the nitty-gritty of modifying Fitzpatrick's prose to better reflect Orr's cause. I was staggered when I chanced upon this document, Brian Fitzpatrick being something of a hero of mine. But I was used to Eddy's excessive long-windedness and idiosyncrasies and decided this was another case of overzealous bad manners. Not at all. When I got around to re-reading the *Meanjin* review I discovered that Fitzpatrick incorporated most of Eddy's suggestion, either in spirit or word for word.

Eddy was concerned that Fitzpatrick had referred to him as Orr's friend 'as if the argument arose from friendship', and he wanted the review to make clear that he did not write the book as a friend of Orr. Fitzpatrick obliged by writing: 'this is not special pleading in the case of putting up the best case for a friend.' Brian Fitzpatrick knew full well that Orr had been intimately involved in this book, yet he writes of the book as if it has appeared unheralded out of the left field, praising 'the high standard of its sustained critical analysis' and how 'above all it bears the stamp of truth, of utter conviction.' Panzee knew what he was talking about when he told Eddy of Fitzpatrick's 'keenness to help' the Orr cause.[196] Another, equally significant, change involved Suzanne Kemp's evidence. In his original Fitzpatrick had described the evidence against Orr being 'in the form of an adolescent girl's diaristic and other annotations of her lovelife'. Eddy was having none of this. He insisted it was not her diary; nor her lovelife. 'It would be more accurate if it read thus; "in the form of what were alleged to be an adolescent girl's diary"; the essential point is that "diary" "annotation" and "lovelife" were all spurious'. Fitzpatrick's review refers only to 'the girl's shifting, uncorroborated and internally inconsistent accounts'; no diary; no letters; no lovelife.[197]

Another thing which struck me about the reviews of *Orr* was that the overseas reviews were remarkably similar, as if they had been written from a supplied critical crib. In England, Ireland, Canada, New Zealand and the United States, Orr was hailed as Australia's Dreyfus. All the reviews emphasised the massive documentation of the case for Orr's innocence and, interestingly, nearly all quote Eddy's introductory remark 'it was not as a friend of Professor Orr I set out to write this book.' I wondered if Montrose had any qualms about his review for the *University Quarterly* which largely followed the form and also emphasised that Eddy was no friend of Orr—knowing him to be a collaborator. The reviewer in the mainstream journal the *New Statesman* appears to have actually read the book. 'As one ploughs on through page after page of unravelled accusation,' he wrote, 'one cannot help feeling he must be overdoing it.'

A lot of effort had gone into securing laudatory reviews; but it wasn't always successful. Alf Conlon, who had long played a backseat role in the Orr camp, was especially active. He had used his considerable contacts to secure a major spread on the book from the *Sydney Morning Herald.* Eddy and Orr had wanted to met the editor and talk about the book, but Conlon wisely decided that their combined looniness would do the cause no good at all. Hopes for 'a big splash' were dashed with the opening paragraph's of Angus Maude's review: 'Mr Eddy says he has tried hard to set down facts objectively and dispassionately. It must be said at once that he has not succeeded.' Angus Maude was smartly consigned to the ranks of those corrupted by the enemy, along with that turncoat Donald Horne, who reviewed the book, as a product of 'a kind of paranoid fallacy' for the *Bulletin* on 31 May. No amount of vituperative letters to the editor could counteract the effect of these negative reviews.

Increasingly, the trio was forced to rely on student papers, several of which ran the same silly review from Dennis Grace, originally in *Tharunka*, who called the book 'one of the most important documents in the history of free communities', referring to its analysis of 'the most cunning and thoroughly executed process of framing in this country'. Bill Ginnane, recently returned from Oxford, weighed in with equally over-the-top rhetoric in the small Catholic paper, *Prospect.* Eddy drew the line at the involvement of *Tribune*, angry that Orr, who had always insisted on the similarities between communist framings and his own case, should want 'a book at my expense, for the communist paper'. Had he taken leave of his critical faculties? 'Have you been immersed for too long, Syd?' he wondered.[198] Ironically, *Tribune* did run a series of articles in defence of Orr.

Within weeks of its publication, Panzee realised that no one was reading *Orr.* Even those who bought it hadn't ploughed through it. After two months sales dwindled to a trickle. What was needed was a shortened version designed to 'avoid argument in full-plain straight slugging ... I would cut out social analysis and ideals in the same way.' What people needed to be told was 'if you leave him in, you'll go in yourself.' For this job, tentatively titled *Orr Summarised*, Panzee suggested the helpful Brian Fitzpatrick.[199]

In some ways Eddy may have been relieved that people were not reading the book, because he suffered terrible fears that he would be sued over it. His fears increased alarmingly once Orr took a writ against Isles one step further in the New South Wales Supreme Court, thereby breaking his promise to Eddy not to do so. Presumably he was unaware that Panzee and Orr had hopes of action over the book, as a way of getting back into court. Some time in 1961, Panzee paid a visit, out of the blue, to Edwin Tanner, ostensibly to acquaint him with libellous allegations that were being made about Tanner in Eddy's book. Tanner felt the intention was to get him to sue, a belief shared by Tanner's wife and son who had been listening in the kitchen.

Tanner was disturbed by this intrusion, but his account of it displays his distinctive, quirky response. He had found the professor's allusions puzzling, especially when Panzee said 'we have trouble with women.' Tanner 'assured him I was not to be included in the class of we's, for women do not trouble me at all.' Panzee explained that he meant professors, and medical men, of which he was both, had trouble with women who wanted to seduce them. Failing to see what this had to do with false statements being published about himself, Tanner felt perhaps he should be jealous:

> I had finer looking features than Professor Wright and no woman had ever seduced me although, since coming to Melbourne one woman did hold my tie at a social gathering ... I am not expressing scorn for physicians or for professors. I have met quite a number of professors in my time and have a great admiration for most of them. I have a great admiration for our family physician. I must ask a few of these about troubles with women.[200]

After seeing Panzee out, Tanner made a vow not to read the book, and he never did. It is not certain whether advances of this kind were made to any other persons who rated adverse comment in the book. Certainly Milanov was too scared to sue: Suzanne and Geoffrey Allison had already shown they were not going to sue; and members of the university council were not about to give Orr another soapbox.

Writs were flying in every direction during 1960 and 1961, unknown to Eddy. As well as suing Isles, Panzee thought it prudent to put pressure on Macbeath as well. Throughout 1960 he was concerned at certain 'slanders' coming from Macbeath regarding Orr's previous academic history and his qualifications. In a letter to Stout in September 1960, Macbeath expressed concern that in his application to Tasmania Orr had given a long list of prizes and scholarships 'not awarded in the three years I was at Belfast'. Orr also laid claim to an MA with honours, but

> no Honours were awarded at Queen's ... and in any case Orr would not have got honours because I have a clear recollection of J Russell, Dr Selincourt and myself deliberating for some time whether the degree should be awarded ... I made it clear to him that he would have to do a good deal better if he were to get a second degree.

The PhD had been submitted twice, unsatisfactorily, Macbeath added.[201]

Some members of the academic staff at the University of New England were also alarmed at what they felt were defamations from Macbeath. Apparently he had told several people that Orr had lied about his qualifications in his applications and that sexual laxity was typical of Orr before he came to Australia.[202] Panzee was incensed. 'I propose to give Macbeath a serious lesson in manners,' he wrote to Stout in London. He promptly had a defamation writ served on the guest professor. He also wrote a stinging letter to another of Orr's referees, Sir David Lindsay Keir, Master of Balliol College. To Stout he suggested calling on Keir at Balliol 'and let him know what you think of it'.[203] Unfortunately, Stout did just that, finding to his utter embarrassment that Keir confirmed Macbeath's opinion, and more. 'I'm sorry you were not warned of Keir,' wrote Panzee 'but I had no basis to believe he was 100% the other way. Syd had assured me their relations were good.'[204]

Even this setback did not give Panzee pause in his desire to teach people lessons. He still saw no reason to doubt Orr's word and made inquiries of another of Orr's referees, JN Wright of St Andrews. When Wright revealed himself intent on 'slandering' Orr, Panzee frightened the life out of him by taking out a defamation writ in the Edinburgh court. In Britain professors were unused to being served with writs. Macbeath was equally nonplussed at impending legal action, reacting, so Panzee gleefully reported, 'by going red then white and grinding his teeth'.[205]

In November another member of staff at New England, intrigued by rumours, received a copy of Orr's qualifications from Belfast which confirmed Macbeath's assertion that Orr did not have an MA with honours and that a PhD had been denied for his thesis on Plato. Once again Panzee took a very dim view of this clandestine activity and the breach of confidentiality. It was the same old story, he told Orr: 'The accuser has really the sympathy of the onlooker because he (treacherously) gets in the first hit.'[206] Others were not so sure. 'The whole of this degree business is very complicated' was the opinion of John Bishop, who also felt that 'a clever lawyer acting on Macbeath's behalf might prove a formidable combination that would do no good to Syd.'[207]

And what did Orr have to say about these allegations concerning his past? He denied them of course, just as he denied having sex in the sand dunes with one of his students. Nevertheless, he did not act on Panzee's suggestion that he insist the university produce his original application. Later, when Panzee had himself seen this application, he reacted with outrage at the suggestion that the university permit anyone to see it.

Early in 1961 Panzee received from Wright's lawyers in Scotland a collection of documents relating to the termination of Orr's employment at St Andrews. From that point nothing more was heard about 'the Macbeath defamations'. I have seen nothing to suggest that Panzee ever discussed the St Andrews affair with Orr and the documents relating to it remained secure among Panzee's papers where I was to find them, to my amazement, some thirty years later. So effective was the process of repressing the stories of Orr's past that I had no expectation that such documents might exist. Indeed, at first I thought these letters belonged to the Australian controversy because so much of the circumstances and special pleading was familiar. It was only when I looked at the date of a letter from Orr describing his personal distress at being unemployed while his position remained vacant, that I realised he was describing a circumstance over a decade earlier. Orr's life had repeated itself at the other end of the world, it seemed, only this time around Orr had the unstoppable Panzee on his side.

As far as Panzee was concerned, allegations about Orr's academic past had nothing to do with the dismissal from Tasmania and was of no consequence, which sits oddly with his enthusiasm for suing anyone who raised issues about this past. It was still the case that he and Orr found these 'diversionary tactics' had a way of tripping them up. Things were going great guns, in April 1961, with the book about to be released, glowing reviews written, Isles on the back foot in the New South Wales courts and Orr set up to do another 'Meet the Press' on television. Orr was doing very well in front of the cameras until a journalist reading from his application asked if he would stand by his statement about his qualifications. Orr was dumbstruck, but Panzee, in the wings, was on his feet and in front of the cameras in a flash, demanding the show stop then and there. 'I have never felt so furious in my life,' he told Stout, 'as to what I consider to be a betrayal of trust of the University of Tasmania. As I saw old Syd on his own in the cameras ... I saw the whole horror of McCarthy.'[208] Later, Orr and Panzee, in company with their lawyer, viewed the programme and threatened a lawsuit if it went to air. HSV7 screened the show, including the offending question on qualifications and Panzee's histrionic response. It made for very memorable television.

In Panzee's view Orr's qualifications, or lack of them, were quite irrelevant to the Kemp issue, which is remarkable given that he always insisted the Orr case was about academic integrity. There were those who felt otherwise. Donald Horne was one. In the *Bulletin* on 2 September, he wondered what FCUSA thought about this since 'it must clearly now consider Mr Orr is a liar.' If he could lie about his qualifications, Horne wondered, was he worthy of membership of the community of scholars? Surely the federal council 'would have some strong opinions on the necessity of men to be honest in their application for academic positions'.

Well, FCUSA did have an opinion. The executive wrote several strongly worded letters to Isles protesting that the university had breached confidentiality by giving details of Orr's application to the media. Immediately on the heels of the protest, in August 1961, the censure of the university, adopted the previous year, began to appear quarterly in the FCUSA journal, *Vestes*. It was also widely publicised overseas and was printed regularly in the *Times Educational Supplement*.

Like Donald Horne, I wonder about the contradictory attitude of those who wanted to censure the university but had no criticism to make of Orr's fraudulent application. There is no room for doubt, the application deliberately and consistently misrepresented Orr's record. A letter from the registrar at Queen's in 1961 made some telling observations. Between the years 1936–39, Orr claimed he had been awarded the class prize in logic, philosophy, ethics, political philosophy, metaphysics, history of philosophy, Greek and mathematics. The registrar observes: 'there is no record as far as I can trace of Mr Orr having been granted the above class prizes,' although he did receive a certificate of distinction, along with other students, in his philosophy subjects. Orr claimed also to have been awarded a two-year foundation scholarship in 1937 of which the registrar could find no record. He noted that awards were made to three other students and it was 'unlikely that Mr Orr would have achieved the standard ... to justify the award'. Nor did he win, as he claimed, the Blayney Exhibition in 1939, although he did win a prize for philosophy, as claimed. Orr's application states he was awarded an MA with first-class honours. 'This statement is incorrect,' says the registrar. 'The calendar lists his award as a Master of Arts.'[209] In his teaching record he claims to have given lectures in five separate subjects. Again the registrar doubted this was true. Another member of Queen's, John Montrose, was able to shed light on this issue, when he was quizzed by Stout. 'I'm not sure what is wrong,' he wrote. 'Orr gave no lectures at Queen's.'[210]

As extra-mural activities Orr claimed membership of the Northern Ireland Council for Social Welfare and the Youth Committee. According to various people associated with these organisations there was no record of his involvement. 'I have never heard his name mentioned,' said the secretary to the Council. As for the Youth Committee, the registrar was able to pass on the comment 'You have therefore, four people ... who have been associated with youth organizations for some time and none of us has ever heard of S.S. Orr.' Orr's inclusion of these imaginary activities was not mere padding. He knew that the chancellor at the time, Sir John Morris, would decide the chair and he was especially interested in community development, wanting a professor who would work for the moral welfare of the community.

I asked one of Orr's most fervent supporters about this application when he was giving me a discourse on academic principles. Without hesitation he said: 'Everybody does it, well I haven't, but it happens all the time.'[211] Just as they get off with their students, I was tempted to say. He agreed that he had known about this deception, that Orr's close associates all knew, but that it had nothing to do with the principle they were supporting. Academic principle is a slippery concept.

Eddy at least understood it would have some bearing on principle, if Orr got back into court. 'If you were scared of the defamation in the *Bulletin* look what you'll be facing if they get a chance in court.'[212] Panzee eventually came to the same conclusion, writing to Orr's lawyer that 'You, Syd and I know he made the same claims for himself in his application to Adelaide. These would come out in a court case whether or not Orr was put in the box. They would ruin him.'[213]

Although he never gave any indication to Orr, I have seen evidence that Panzee investigated Orr's original application to Melbourne, so he would have known that Orr had included old references from Professors Wright and Macbeath, despite their specific refusal to be referees. I believe that Boyce Gibson found out about this deception and that this, along with trouble within the department at Melbourne, may have caused his enmity toward Orr. The ruinous element in all these misleading applications was not simply that Orr was given to falsehoods, trouble enough in itself, but that he was willing to consistently flout a sacrosanct academic principle of the community of scholars. Consider the rhetoric of some of the Orr cheer squad in full indignation. Was not the University of Tasmania being condemned, censured, maligned, because it had failed to meet the accepted standards of the community of scholars? Had not the university been excommunicated because it could not be said to meet the basic requirement of the community of scholars—'a community of persons disposed in such a way that they are able to pursue the truth in the various academic disciplines at the highest possible level'?[214] John Polya put the case most forcefully in *Vestes* in 1962, saying: 'Men [*sic*] whose purpose is to discover and preserve and transmit truth form the universities in the older sense. They are scholars, specialists in truth, the same way as knights are specialists in war, merchants specialists in money and cobblers specialists in shoes.' After sacking Orr the University of Tasmania could lay no claim to being a true university or its staff members of the community of scholars, in Polya's view: 'To teach and live in the service of an ephemeral club or party gives one the habit of half-truths, which will not survive the whims of those who like to guard their tame professors as they used to guard their fathers' pigs.' Orr himself, when asked how he could work with his ex-colleagues if he were reinstated, responded loftily 'In a university, one pursues truth, one does not work with people.'[215] It stands to reason, surely, that a basic requirement of men whose purpose is to 'discover, preserve and transmit truth' is that they do not lie when seeking admittance to the 'community dedicated to truth'. What appears plain as day to me seems to have escaped the notice of the scholars who imposed bans and censures. They were not prepared to talk about it whilst riding their high horse of principle, that is for sure!

In Hobart, despite censure and bans and lawsuits and bad press, the university determined to batten down and ride out the storm. The appointment of James McAuley to a readership in poetry at the university was a considerable academic coup in the face of the censure. Support from influential commentators such as Peter Coleman and Donald Horne at the *Bulletin* was encouraging, as was the mounting disquiet among mainland academics who felt that the Orr case was a bottomless pit. One academic who had grown heartily sick of the issue and the way in which it had crowded out so many other pressing staff association issues year in and year out was Ken Buckley, who was retiring as secretary of FCUSA in June 1961. No doubt he could have done without a letter he received in his official capacity, from a Miss G, an academic in England, but once a student of Orr's at St Andrews. This letter, dated 31 March 1961, was sent in response to an announcement of the censure in the *Times*

Educational Supplement. As Miss G explained, seeing the censure had jolted her into exposing her own unhappy association with Orr:

> I was an undergraduate at St Andrews, Fife, from 1942–1945 and a student of Mr Orr (as he was then) for logic in the session 1944–45. Although in my final year I was only 18, Mr Orr had left his wife behind in Belfast and made a determined effort to seduce me within weeks of our first meeting. His line of attack was originally very corrupting, consisting entirely of praise of sex in the abstract, which had a lubricious effect but did not seem to put one in any immediate danger. However I did in fact have to fight him good and hard one night on the golf course in order to resist his advances—he kept muttering that he'd never had to force a woman yet, but I was under the decided impression that he was using force on me and was very frightened indeed. I got back to my residence in a very distressed condition but decided against complaining to the university authorities on the grounds that it would make me look a complete fool to say that I had genuinely thought he wanted to talk about soil erosion on the cliffs at 11 o'clock at night. This was the argument he had first used on me when I expressed surprise at his advances and at that age it did not occur to me that a University might prefer to protect me rather than mock me for my naivete.
>
> The class he gave in Psychology to the second year Philosophy students caused considerable embarrassment to at least one of them because he insisted in describing experiments which he alleged to have conducted at Belfast (this may not be true of course) with male and female students in completely darkened rooms to see whether tactile stimuli were as effective

> sexually when detached from personal associations. He swore his class to silence on this, but it got out and there was considerable hostility to him in the university. He had been promised verbally a lectureship after a year as an assistant and the promise was not kept so that for a time he was receiving unemployment benefits. His wife was with him by then and he professed to be an utterly reformed character, 'grown up' as he put it, so that I was delighted to hear of his appointment to the antipodes. However now that events have shown he was not in fact reformed I think it is my duty to say that his past at St Andrews confirms the rightness of the University of Tasmania in protecting students from him.

The letter had first come to Melbourne University and been inadvertently opened by the staff association secretary, Don Mackay, an enthusiastic Orr supporter. He had passed in on with the aside that 'it may be true, but it is irrelevant' and promised not to breathe a word about it.

Buckley responded to the letter by sending a copy of *Vestes* with the report of the committee of inquiry established by FCUSA. Miss G's reply was gracious, but highly critical, and she remained entirely unconvinced that the extreme stand taken was justified by apparent procedural deficiencies: 'The point on which I originally wrote to you, namely that Professor Orr was not a person fitted to be a university professor by virtue of his past record, has been utterly lost sight of in the technicalities of legalism.' Buckley replied for a second time, saying:

> You believe Orr to be a person unfitted to be a university professor by virtue of his past record. If you will forgive me for saying so, your personal reason for believing this rests upon the information of your untested statement ... if I believed Orr to be guilty of what

> was alleged ... then I would agree he is unfitted to be a university professor. In fact I do not know whether he is guilty.

Wishing to rid himself of the responsibility of this correspondence, as well as the executive position at FCUSA, Buckley sent the letters to Panzee explaining that 'The enclosed correspondence should be disposed of lest it get into the wrong hands. The correspondence speaks for itself. My main concern was to placate the lady so she would not spread her story further. In that I think I succeeded ... It seems to me you will be the safest repository, leaving no trace of it in the Federal Council files.'[216] So, ironic though it may be, it is thanks to Panzee's meticulous approach to documentation that I was able to stumble upon this letter, which was corroborated, quite unprompted, by another ex-student from St Andrews. Both are strikingly similar to the story told by Suzanne Kemp; the golf course in St Andrews being the equivalent of the hills above Hobart where Orr took Suzanne, and tried to take another student, Patricia Ure, 'to see the lights'—a bit more interesting, perhaps, than soil erosion on the cliffs of Fife, but the intention seems the same.

There is no evidence that Miss G's claims were discussed among the Orr supporters or with the man himself. There was never a question that it would be used as Miss G intended: to be tabled at a FCUSA meeting so as to alert the academic community to Orr's previous misdemeanours.

Is this called suppression of evidence, or merely prudence? Buckley has since pointed out that if the press in Australia had learned about the alleged earlier seduction it would have been sensationalised—an undesirable and pointless outcome. 'On the other hand,' he writes, 'I did not act as censor. The lady in London was free to communicate with the press or the university if she wished. She chose not to do so and I was happy to see the matter left at that.'[217]

Maybe so. But I can just imagine the kind of invective such

action would inspire if it were the University of Tasmania dealing with sensitive correspondence in this manner. I guess it comes down to the primitive concept of fighting fire with fire. If you believe you are faced with a conspiracy of major proportions using dubious and immoral tactics, then you may feel compelled to use similar tactics in response—stooping to the level of the unscrupulous enemy.

This point was made in a generally sympathetic article on the Orr case in the *Bulletin* of 1 February 1961 by journalist Andrew Dorset, who considered that five years down the track the case threatened to disintegrate into 'a sad and endless spectacle of smearing and counter smearing, paranoia and intrigue'. A detached keeper of the score card for unsavoury tactics, Dorset conceded, 'would probably award top marks to the Orr party'. He was unconvinced the pro-Orr tactics were necessitated by 'a conspiracy against them so sinister and complicated that what seems like a disgraceful smear is in fact a simple truth'. Dorset did accept the good faith of Orr and his closest associates that 'the university's conduct is only part of a vast conspiracy involving the whole of the Tasmanian "ruling class"—a conspiracy that has introduced brainwashing into Australia and does not hesitate at murder.' In the Orr camp, Dorset concluded, 'Every principle of justice, liberty and human dignity compels them to go on fighting if totalitarian dictatorship, brainwashing and assassination are not to become normal parts of Australian life.' When these were the odds, principles might have to be bent more than just a little.

But didn't they claim that the threat to democracy and human dignity was most acute if the principles of the academy were undermined? I can take the words directly from Orr himself, published in *Diogenes* in September 1961:

> If the policy of an institution is based on deception and suppression for the maintenance of falsehood, how can you prevent this same flavour from contam-

> inating the 'scholarly' work of the institution ... if members of the institution condone the policy based on lies and suppression to maintain justice, how far can their brother scholars in the 'commonwealth of learning' trust them?

CHAPTER NINE

They can get out of it with some shreds of reputation left

'God save us from academics—they are right out of this world' exploded Orr in 1964, furious that after nearly nine years of struggling mightily, the academic community was not prepared to go out on a limb and get him an academic job. Almost everyone felt the full force of his bile, but none more than the executive members of FCUSA who, apart from being willing to sell him out, were stingy with their financial support. Instead of helping him, they were 'setting up their offices and paying a new executive secretary whose sole job it is to get higher wages for the boys—hence they want to be rid of unimportant things like the Orr case'.[218] Stout fared little better, with Orr fuming about him that 'coping with the stupidity of our alleged supporters is as difficult as handling manoeuvres of the enemy.'[219] Panzee, on leave in England in 1964, was on the receiving end of pages and pages of closely typed vitriolic diatribe, from which he alone was exempt.

Orr's grief and rage was fuelled by his realisation that both the Association of Philosophers and FCUSA were unwilling to insist on his reinstatement or force the university to pay for another equivalent job elsewhere. 'Without a job a man remains a parasite and pariah,' he wrote in a poignant plea to Panzee. 'He is no longer an individual at all, less a human being and therefore like a yapping dog—the butt of every foul foot.'[220] It was inconceivable to him that he might not once again be a professor and that the university might not be made to rescind the judgement against him. That his academic supporters were prepared to throw in the towel far short of his goal was a bitter pill he did not intend to swallow.

The first to show a weakening of resolve were the philosophers. It had never been envisaged that the boycott on the chair would go on and on, and by 1962 Stout had real fears that philosophy might evaporate in Tasmania. He held firmly to the opinion that it was necessary to get Orr out of Hobart and get 'someone really good appointed to the Chair'.[221] Since he felt Orr should never have been appointed in the first place, he was not about to insist he be reinstated. In any case, Orr had repeatedly assured the philosophers that he did not seek reinstatement and had an urgent desire to leave Tasmania. But after six years he was still there and Stout was not sanguine about his chances of a job elsewhere.

Professor Arthur Fox from the University of Western Australia succeeded Macbeath as the visiting professor in Hobart in 1961–62 and he had proposed that a subcommittee of Stout, Passmore and himself consider how the boycott might be lifted. Once in Hobart his support for the boycott rapidly expired. He wrote to Stout of the overwhelming feeling of distaste for Orr at the university, of what he heard about Orr's appalling personal reputation and the fact that church support for his 'new evidence' had quite disappeared. 'The philosophers' adverse pronouncements of which I was a signatory,' he complained 'was based only on the supposed relevance of the "new evidence",' which was now shown to be illusory. He attacked Ginnane for his over-the-top pronouncements on Orr and 'far too much and too incredible puffing up of Orr as a moral hero and competent academic (with a shortage of adequate evidence) and too little readiness to admit the good faith, knowledge of fact, and accuracy of judgement among those who would regard Orr's reinstatement with dismay'. He was also shocked and pained by the 'cruel and unwarranted vilification of Milanov'.[222]

By 1962 then, it was clear to Stout and other philosophers, if not Ginnane, that if the chair were to be filled, Orr would have to be found a position of some kind elsewhere. The idea of jointly creating a job for Orr was raised with Isles informally in August that year and discussions were held with the vice-chancellor of the University of New South Wales, Professor Baxter, who had suggested that Orr might be appointed as the assistant editor of a new publication to be called *Australian University*. Isles was cautiously open to the suggestion, whereas Stout was less than enthusiastic. 'I don't like this job much,' he wrote to Panzee, 'for I never like the choice of evils which is what we are faced with now.'[223] Panzee wasn't happy either. He did not like the idea of creating special jobs and he certainly didn't want the philosophers to change their stance on the chair. Besides, he remained concerned about the continued presence of Milanov, 'who stands condemned of grossly unacademic conduct. Can anyone recommend a new professor be put in peril by him?'[224]

Stout continued to shop around. At New England he was told that the classics department might take Orr as a lecturer in Plato provided that his salary was paid and that the position was supernumerary. The professor of philosophy wasn't at all enthusiastic. 'If he were a good philosopher I'd be happy to have him, but I can't and won't carry another passenger.' Another professor 'Wouldn't have Syd at any price.'[225] The general opinion was that no university would give Orr a teaching job, even though most agreed that 'Syd is unlikely to be such a bloody fool as to make *that* mistake twice.'[226] In 1963 Professor Thornton, at the University of New South Wales, said he might take Orr but only as a supernumerary with his salary paid from elsewhere. But there was no one to pay the salary. Isles had made no commitment and FCUSA was very dubious that academics would be prepared to put their hands in their pockets to create a job for Orr.

The executive members of FCUSA were also less than determined in support of Orr. Almost as soon as censure was formally applied they were looking for ways in which it might be lifted. While they had agreed to some form of financial assistance to

Orr (Panzee suggested £200 per month) they felt 'it is in his best interests to seek another position' and undertook 'to give him all possible support in this enterprise'. Their lukewarm support was influenced in no small way by his legal action against Isles which they were not prepared to support or condone, citing legal advice that the action 'would almost certainly fail'.[227] At the annual meeting of FCUSA in August 1962 it was agreed that the censure could be lifted if the University of Tasmania adopted an acceptable tenure statute. The executive was also empowered to negotiate a position, such as that suggested by Baxter, to rehabilitate Orr.

At its meeting in the same month, the Association of Philosophers also agreed it would withdraw its ban if the university adopted standards and procedures for dismissal as well as making an *ex gratia* payment to Mrs Orr and help in securing a suitable post for Orr. A year later this 'suitable post' had failed to materialise, leading political scientist Peter Boyce to wonder in *Crux* magazine 'is it not surprising that from all the mainland cannon-fire one cannot find any public *promise* of a position for Orr. Could it be mainland agitators are not really anxious to accommodate Orr within their own institutions?'

In Tasmania it was apparent to a number of senior academics, including McAuley, now professor of English, that a settlement involving some financial payment to Orr must be achieved. 'It was a pretty hard road to travel because the divisions were terribly deep,' McAuley recalled.[228] Nevertheless the staff association was able to present a tenure statute to council in late 1962 which went through a gruesome process of eight drafts in the following six months. In July 1963, in the wake of a resolution from the philosophers to get the chair in Hobart filled, the acting vice-chancellor was prepared to meet with Stout to discuss a possible settlement. For some months meetings continued between representatives from the university, Stout, Ginnane, FCUSA president and secretary, and Panzee, to hammer out a draft settlement. It was agreed that the university would enact a proper tenure statute and dismissal procedures. It also would publicly admit that some procedures used in the internal inquiry might have been unsatisfactory and that it might have erred in summarily dismissing Orr. The university agreed to make a payment of about £16 000 to Orr. In return the censure and bans were to be withdrawn, as was the legal action against Isles, and Orr was to give an undertaking not to seek reinstatement nor to apply for a position at the University of Tasmania. These last two requirements were appended in confidential clauses to the agreement.

Such a settlement did not suit Orr. 'We agreed,' he remonstrated with Panzee, 'that any settlement in Hobart should agree on *actual* reinstatement and *formal vacation of the judgement.* No mere public statement ... will meet the bill for me.'[229] In this he probably had the support of no one but Ginnane. By now even Panzee was looking for a settlement along with the rest. So at the final meeting on 10 December he agreed, on Orr's behalf, to the terms of settlement, but only reluctantly agreed to advise Orr not to seek reinstatement.

December 1963 was a period of high drama for all involved. On the 13th the settlement was rammed through the university council at an uproarious meeting, later referred to as a palace revolution. Two days later five hard-line conservative members of the council, including the chancellor, resigned in loud protest which was captured in bold *Mercury* headlines. Readers of the *Mercury* were even more taken aback to see on 16 December a remarkable public statement from the university saying that 'in the best interests of the university' they would now defer to the view that 'we acted wrongly in terminating the appointment of Professor Orr as we did.' All through the day there were news flashes expectant of a response from Orr, then in Sydney. He apparently was caught totally unawares—for some inexplicable reason Panzee had failed to communicate to him the university's final offer. Orr rang at 7 am on the 17th to tell the staff association he would not accept without reinstatement. They were puzzled and angry. Hadn't Panzee agreed to this settlement on Orr's behalf? In the press Orr was quoted as saying he would not accept 'for a million pounds ... I am not interested in money.' The *Mercury* published a statement from Orr's Sydney lawyer that Orr would not accept which was promptly denied in a telegram from Orr to the university saying: 'We agree to a conference.'

By this time it was felt all the conferences had been held and resolution had to be immediate. The press carried angry denunciations of Orr from his erstwhile allies, increasing the pressure on him to near breaking point. Orr spent the time on the phone and in frantic conferences. At 7 pm on the 19th, after five and a half hours negotiation at Sydney University, Orr agreed, reluctantly, to accept. Weary and disheartened, he made a statement to the waiting journalist, saying he had been 'persuaded to sign in the best interests of the university staff and students'. He released his own unacceptable counter-proposal for scrutiny. As for the money: 'It is big enough to be symbolic—I will not haggle,' he said.

'He'll take cash' screamed the headlines of the *Advocate*, while others in more tasteful headlines proclaimed that the Orr case was over, triggering jubilation in some quarters, dismay in others. For Stout it was 'the end of eight years hard'. In Hobart the settlement came to many as a complete shock. Aware of the insult to Edwin Tanner, Gwen Harwood wrote to him: 'If anyone had told me a week ago the university would give money to that ratbag I would have laughed them to scorn ... this business has knocked the stuffing right out of us. We'll probably be found gibbering in the corner reading Noddy books and passing each other 16 000 in play-money.'[230] McAuley, who had been much involved in the negotiations, bore the brunt of some pretty hostile reactions from those who felt he, who knew that Orr was a fraud, 'had twiced on them'. He had to 'privately explain that I was in a terribly difficult situation and if they didn't like it, too bad'.[231] In England the University of Tasmania's assistant registrar Tony Kearney heard of the settlement on the BBC news, to his enormous relief. He, along with many other academics in England, sent telegrams of congratulations. At the other extreme, Emeritus Professor Taylor resigned his lifelong membership of the staff association in protest at the 'malicious libel and gross exaggeration' that Orr had been instrumental in the royal commission and had been dismissed for that reason. 'I instigated the Royal Commission,' he insisted, detailing his meetings with the premier, 'my health was permanently broken by weeks of work and worry.'[232] Townsley too was horrified. I do not know how Mrs Geoffrey Allison reacted to the news.

All the joy and all the anguish and all the recrimination was in vain. When it came to the crunch and Orr was presented with a legal document, he would not sign. Gerald Firth, who had gone to enormous lengths on behalf of the staff association to engineer this settlement, was infuriated. 'As usual Orr is the nigger,' he wrote to Dallas, 'you may now rely on me to be sensible about that little bastard. I've done my best to get him a settlement and when all is said and done 16 000 pounds is a fair swag of money. Now it has been thrown back in our faces, he's on his own.'[233]

Orr would settle for nothing less than reinstatement. In this he was encouraged by philosopher Sandy Anderson (son of John Anderson) who urged him to stand alone and be a martyr rather than capitulate to pressure. Another enthusiast was philosopher Ruth Walker, the sole woman to register strong public support, who briefly entered the fray with a long diatribe in *Nation* accusing Stout of selling out. Stout was having none of it. The settlement might be flawed, but as far as he and the great bulk of the philosophy profession were concerned, the proposed settlement constituted 'the last chance' for Orr. This was the position both he and Eddy put to Orr, expressing dismay at Panzee's odd behaviour. 'Panzee was bound to incur, if not openly, at any rate privately and in the hearts of many people, the odium of charges of prevarication (if not downright lying) and double dealing (which of course he has incurred),' Stout wrote.[234] It was Eddy's view that Panzee had not told Orr the terms because he knew they would be rejected but expected that once faced with a *fait accompli* Orr would capitulate, seeing that they were really in his best interests.

These private opinions Orr promptly passed on to Panzee whose characteristic response was threats of libel against Stout and 'his defamatory pals'.[235] He maintained the agreement as presented was 'so far away from what I undertook to recommend Syd accept' that they must get expert legal advice about its content. Stout, anxious to placate his volatile associate in arms, agreed. Inevitably the whole settlement bogged down in legal process. Advice tendered by law professors Derham and Ford was that the confidential clauses gave the agreement 'doubtful legal standing' and could possibly make the document null and void. Panzee suspected that the documents had deliberately been made legally unacceptable. Both the philosophers and FCUSA decided, on legal advice, that they should not sign an agreement jointly with Orr which might make them party to his action against Isles.

By mid-1964 both academic associations were once more riding the Orr tiger. A long-time supporter from Melbourne, on leave in England, claimed 'I left instructions to my wife that the word Orr ... [was] not to appear in her letters'.[236] In July 1964 Orr's lawyers had resubmitted his terms for settlement to Isles, with the threat that Orr would escalate his legal action against Isles if they were not accepted. Prior to the meetings of both the Association of Philosophers and FCUSA in Brisbane in August Orr had issued writs against Isles in every other state and writs against the Tasmanian government printer as well. The total amount claimed was close to half a million pounds, a staggering amount of money in 1964.

Stout continued to have no success on the job front. The notion of a senior research job in classics at Newcastle received cold water from the professor there: 'In the current circumstances I cannot urge you too strongly the vital necessity of pressing for Orr's restoration ... into the Tasmanian Chair.'[237] For his part Orr would only accept nominal reinstatement, or professor emeritus, plus eight years of professorial salary to be paid to another university to create a professorial post. It was all pie in the sky and Stout knew it. The University of Tasmania would never reinstate Orr, and nor should it, in his opinion. Orr would be lucky to get a tutorship. At the philosophers' August meeting David Armstrong, in a gesture of conciliation, offered a tutorship at Sydney, only to be staunchly opposed by the other delegates from that same university. Another offer came from Tasmania that if any university would be prepared to grant study leave to one of its senior teachers of philosophy to take up a visiting appointment for three years at Tasmania, then Orr could rehabilitate himself in the temporary position created elsewhere.[238] This proposal did not even get the time of day. No university was going to forfeit a senior position in order to get Orr in return.

There was a suggestion that Orr should not have to compete for an academic job, to which both Panzee and Stout were implacably opposed. Stout felt that it was 'academically wrong to make appointments on any ground other than academic merit'. There, as far as Orr was concerned, was the rub. Stout was not alone in his low opinion of Orr's academic worth, but even if he were to put aside his concerns that Orr's philosophy was confused and 'airy fairy', Orr had published no academic work since 1951, and that had been a very minor contribution. The oft-mentioned work on Plato, which supposedly required only a little time to complete, had never materialised. In a poignant and unusually realistic appraisal of his circumstances, Orr laid out his disadvantages:

> there are two court judgments that can be quoted ... lack of recent publications, alleged loss through want of practice of professional competence, risk of un-

> balance through long obsession with private wrongs and the principles of the case, the absence by death or alienation of most of my distinguished supporters or administrative referees, and even age ... not to mention the fact that my special field of research is now thought ... to be out of the current stream and unproductive.

Surely Panzee could see that for FCUSA 'to leave an academic in such circumstances to rely on appointment in the normal way is to throw him to the wolves after benefiting from his struggle ... to enhance their own security.'[239] He wanted a personal chair created for him. Panzee was not swayed on this most important principle that an academic job could only be awarded on academic merit. He was 'unequivocally against the proposal' and would have no part in 'pressures to secure an academic appointment which you would not get under academic merits'.[240] Stalemate.

FCUSA had pretty well had Orr. At a meeting in August 1964 it was agreed that the settlement with the University of Tasmania would be renegotiated; a draft agreement was already drawn up ready for signature. Orr vented his spleen about this turnabout in his letters to Panzee in England. The people on FCUSA were 'hell bent on selling out at any cost' because they felt 'the thing has gone on too long and they want to be rid of it.'[241] He might have expected this, he felt, since the executive had been 'taken over by a young rabble who don't give a damn about academic principles', forgetting perhaps that Panzee himself was on the executive of FCUSA and had persuaded the organisation to pay a supporting allowance of £1000 per year to Mrs Orr.

As he poured out his heart, and his bile, in long, long letters to Panzee, Orr grew increasingly worried about the perfunctory replies or, more usually, the silence. Panzee had recently remarried and this, plus the distance between them, seemed to Orr to mark a cooling in his relationship. 'I am still worried about not hearing from you and hope you have read my letters,' he wrote. He had even heard that Panzee supported the FCUSA settlement proposal: 'I know this to be untrue and impossible ... but I must say I am utterly bewildered.'[242]

Not only the academic community, but even the church had deserted him. Professor Macbeath, a strong Presbyterian, had made his presence felt in the Scots Kirk during his time in Hobart and it had been quite silent on Orr since the first foray into the case in 1958. Disturbed at protests within the church, the Kirk had resolved in December 1958 to 'take no further action in the Orr case and disassociate itself from published statements with regard to same.'[243] The Catholic Archbishop, Guildford Young, once another stalwart, had gone silent as well. As a strong advocate of the need for the church to speak with authority on secular matters, Guildford Young had supported the Kirk inquiry, and its conclusions. Together with Bishop Cranswick he had protested against Reg Wright's using in court confidential documents taken from Cranswick, and urged another inquiry on the university; but following the collapse of the settlement, which both had applauded, Cranswick and Young pointedly withdrew from the debate. Orr believed 'Gillie' had been caught in McAuley's thrall and was 'actively involved with McAuley in an unholy plot to get DLP and catholic control of top posts at the university'.[244]

But Orr still had confidence in the media and the legal threats. *Nation* could be relied upon to run his material, and, he told Panzee, 'I know this bloke McGregor in the SMH who can be relied upon to write stuff.'[245] He also had ideas to turn up the heat on the university in his legal action. 'Can you get in touch with Hector Dunn and find out what he did with the anonymous letter the church got from this bloke in Sydney in 1958.'[246] As part of the push to garner some more 'new evidence', pressure was again applied to the so-called psychiatrist, Dr Engisch, who sent a statement to Orr's solicitor claiming that Orr had told him about Suzanne Kemp and her father. In this statement he described himself as Orr's personal psychiatric advisor, but was still not prepared to say that his client had communicated with him before his dismissal.

It was distasteful to be suing Isles in every state, as well as the United Kingdom and New Zealand, Orr told a worried supporter, but his legal advisors were 'keener than ever to press ahead' since it would give him a legal verdict on Kemp and 'a great deal more money'. His preference was for the university to get him a job, such as a research chair, paid for by them but at another university.[247]

The bloke named McGregor at the *Sydney Morning Herald* may or may not have been a reliable conduit for Orr, but his newspaper ran an extensive story on the collapse of the 1963 settlement which was picked up by nearly every other paper, in August 1964. According to these reports, the university had changed the terms of the settlement and had generally welched on the deal by including legally suspect clauses, which made the settlement 'null and void'. Neither the philosophers nor FCUSA would agree to it, the press reported, implying that the bans would continue. This was too much for McAuley. While he felt the bans had only marginally hurt, he was concerned that 'we were once again slipping back into being the object of detestation' and 'getting near the brink of real damage to the institution'. As chairman of the professorial board he decided 'to take a step which was terribly dangerous'. He had a file full of legal correspondence which showed quite clearly that the university had acted in good faith. He rang the editor or chairman of every major newspaper and sent them numbered photocopies. After a period 'when I really sweated blood the last of those photocopies was returned and the newspaper campaign stopped dead.'[248]

Worse was to come, the realisation of which began to dawn on Orr as he waited in vain to catch the elusive Panzee on his way through Mascot airport in October. It seemed that 'the General of the Army' did not wish to see him. 'If you had said it was your wish to remain incommunicado, or even that for the future your changed circumstances made this necessary I would have understood ... we cannot go on in this way ... I must confess that physically and mentally I've more than had it.'[249] He would have been even more distraught to know that Panzee was actually working with the FCUSA executive to effect another settlement, basically the same as that rejected in 1963.

Orr was curtly informed in November that the documents were to be sent to him to sign within a week. In a series of phone calls Panzee was unambiguously blunt, telling Orr that 'instead of wasting time writing long letters' he should sign or he would be 'going it alone'. Orr could not believe his ears. After eight years 'no-one has been more acutely aware than you of the dangers of wrong procedures and the irreparable harm I have suffered from it,' he told Panzee, who now demanded that Orr accept 'a grossly unfair settlement', because this was his best chance of getting a job. This line was 'the most wicked humbug and casuistry', when the position clearly was that once he settled he was finished. His lawyers too felt that he must not accept and that if he did, out of loyalty to Panzee, he would not get an academic job and 'would have to adjust myself to some other way of life'. Still Panzee was his 'next friend'; he had given huge amounts materially and otherwise to help Orr survive. In the course of the 'prolonged and frightful battle' Orr had gained 'unique affection and admiration' for Panzee and 'could not go on alone without harming you as much as myself'. Bitterly he told Panzee 'if you feel you must go through with this ... go ahead and do so.'[250]

In a more contrite mood, Orr informed Panzee and Stout early in 1965 that he definitely would sign the settlement if they first got him a job. Panzee remained steadfast that it was not on, but Stout once more did a round robin of his philosophical colleagues who had been so determined in their boycott of the chair. What he proposed was far short of Orr's expectations and the funding arrangement unclear—at least part of the salary would have to be raised by academics themselves. He suggested a funded research position, without tenure, which would be supernumerary and not affect the existing staff establishment. The response was almost uniformly negative. Jack Smart at Adelaide was sure that no female student 'could be safer with anyone now than with Orr.'[251] However, he was 'not game to take Orr here, for I feel he would be a difficult colleague and this is a small department—he would be hard to hide.'[252] At Monash, Rankin felt the vice-chancellor would think 'Orr is far too dangerous.'[253] At Melbourne, Boyce Gibson did the honourable thing and spoke to the vice-chancellor, who was not impressed. At New South Wales it was felt that Orr should be in a large department with the head, Hamblin, adding 'I should not like my attitude to be interpreted as outright opposition.'[254] Newcastle, which had promoted a total academic ban on Tasmania, felt it was too small for Orr, and too remote and otherwise unsuitable. From ANU, Passmore was the most candid. 'Quite frankly I do not want Orr here, even gratis, in the situation of almost constant discussion which prevails in this department, he would be nothing but a nuisance. I don't think he has any talent at all for positions he doesn't share ... it's a good idea as long as it isn't here.' To his credit Passmore was willing to acknowledge the hypocrisy of his position that 'in my opinion it is vital that Orr continue his career in philosophy [although] I don't think it would do philosophy any harm if he turned to something else.'[255] So much for the boycotting philosophers.

Only the University of New England offered any prospect. In July 1965 a secret meeting was held between the vice-chancellor of that university and Goddard, professor of philosophy, together with Isles and Carey from Tasmania. It appears to have been totally abortive. Possibly Isles refused to carry the full salary for a position. He certainly had no great hopes for a settlement, having written to his friend Eric Ashby, weeks before, that the case 'looks very unlikely to reach its eventual conclusion, at least in my lifetime. However I have learned to live with it in friendly toleration, and no doubt would feel a sense of bereavement if it were to come suddenly to an end.'[256] Oddly enough there was more positive determination to close the case from the new president of FCUSA, Peter Brett, and from Panzee, who kept trying to get Orr to make a settlement with the university. Panzee had told Orr that his hope of securing an academic position was 'an unattainable aim'. Likewise he warned Orr that he was unlikely to meet success in his case against Isles in the New South Wales courts—that application was sure to destroy him.[257] He was more than disgruntled that Orr's Sydney lawyer, Don Champion, was making all the running and that Orr continually deferred to him, refusing meetings and entries until he had been briefed by 'his legal advisors'. Panzee had told Isles, in a very amicable letter written in 1964, that if a settlement was to be concluded as they both desired, they should be careful about 'the run of the legal fish'.[258] Quite a turnabout for a man whose first recourse was invariably to issue a writ.

Using his still-considerable influence with Orr, Panzee arranged a meeting with Peter Brett in early September 1965, when Orr was in Melbourne. At this meeting, once again, Orr refused to state what his minimum terms might be, at the insistence of his legal advisors, but he did impress on Brett that he had 'important new evidence ... and once this evidence was known to the other side their attitude toward settlement would change.'[259] Orr wanted Brett to arrange a meeting between himself and the University of Tasmania. This Brett duly did.

What followed was a flurry of activity to give some substance to this new evidence, concerning Suzanne Kemp's relationship with her father. After the abortive trip to Sydney in July 1965 to visit the journalist voyeur who had reported seeing the Kemps, both Panzee and journalist John Hayes gave Champion statements about what this man had told them of events witnessed in McLeay Street nine years before,[260] but there was nothing else. For a brief moment there were hopes of a breakthrough concerning the sudden death of Reg Kemp at Orford over two years earlier: John Hayes got it into his head that Kemp might have committed suicide, despite an autopsy report listing his cause of death as a heart attack. Hayes alerted Panzee, who could not resist playing detective, that apparently the body had been removed to Hobart without a death certificate having been signed. Add to this the fact that the body was cremated and ... who knows. Using his contacts in the police force, Panzee got copies of the relevant documents in late September. Finding nothing substantial (although he did note the government pathologist was *the same man* who had doubted Orr's bullet wound!), he then demanded further details of the cremation. In November Panzee wrote to Orr 'I have not yet heard anything from the man in Hobart. I trust you are not relying on evidence from there of McLeay St to get a total reversal.'[261]

Orr was not deflected or deterred. As usual he was sure he was on a winner, as was Champion, who wrote to Panzee worried that he was about to 'sell out' Orr. How could Panzee do this, he wanted to know, with 'the very possibility of obtaining a statement from the Sydney voyeur by inside pressure, we are in the strongest possible position.'[262] Perhaps Champion had deduced what lawyers for Isles had already advised, that it was hard to see how the university could introduce Orr's application into the defamation suit, and that they would have the devil's own job getting Suzanne back into the witness box. It was equally hard to see how anecdotal evidence about Suzanne could be introduced into a defamation case against the vice-chancellor. One would have to say that for a man who had spectacularly lost two court cases, and willingly entertained the idea that judges were the agents of his enemies, Orr had a robust faith in lawyers.

Whatever concerns Isles and his lawyers might have about defending the defamation action, they were not thrown by Orr's 'new evidence'. To quote Brett, who was present at the meeting, 'it was plain from certain things they said to us which I believe would be better not recorded' that they were unimpressed.[263]

There was no question that they intended to change their 1963 offer one iota. In Brett's opinion Orr's only options were to settle for what was offered or fight. Panzee agreed, but reiterated that if Orr were to fight he would lose everything. Panzee guessed, quite rightly, that he too might be severely hurt in the fallout.

In any case Panzee was fed up, telling Champion 'I abhor people who, as soon as they get and give an agreement on a base level then try to raise the price.' Enough was enough. 'I am dammed sick of being shouted at when I do what Syd has agreed to and further what you advised him to do.'[264] There was one other pressing consideration. Panzee knew Orr was critically ill; his heart was so weak he was not long for the world. Having supported Mrs Orr and her children for eight years he was not about to see them left destitute when Orr died, knowing, as he did, Orr's single-minded disregard for his wife's emotional or material needs.

Orr was still hanging out for reinstatement—at least nominal—so that he might be rehabilitated in academic life. His old staff association colleague Gerald Firth was flabbergasted: 'Now that we are sure that Orr's application contained misstatements of a kind that cannot possibly be accidental, how can anyone hope that he be reinstated—*anywhere.*' All that FCUSA could do, Firth believed, was see 'how they can get out of it with some shreds of reputation left'.[265] Most agreed. With Panzee's total co-operation Brett negotiated an agreement with the university on 9 December, to be ratified by the FCUSA special meeting on 14 February 1966. It was understood by Brett, and by the University of Tasmania, that Panzee was acting as Orr's 'next friend' and had authority to negotiate on Orr's behalf. For his part Panzee had a letter from Orr saying 'if you must ... go ahead and do so.'

Characteristically, Orr interpreted the relationship quite differently once the settlement was known to him. Ill he may have been, but he could still get on the phone and write letters to muster a backlash against this 'sellout'. Rumbles of discontent were heard from the remaining pockets of staunch support in Hobart and mainland campuses, invariably coming from new academic warriors who perhaps were unaware that vitriolic personal attack was Orr's staple mode of discourse. Perhaps also they did not know that Panzee, the subject of this attack, had been Orr's life-support system for nearly a decade.

Panzee had planned to fly to Hobart at Christmas to be with the Orr family and talk to Orr about his future but, as he told Sadie Orr, 'week by week there came news of defamation of me by, or inspired by, Syd.'[266] Orr had told people that Panzee's betrayal of him was the worst thing that had ever been done to him. It was typical Orr hyperbole, but Panzee was wounded to the depths of his soul. His own reaction was just as typical: he threatened writs for defamation against Orr. In his defence Panzee also distributed a four-page memorandum to staff associations explaining that his actions, and those of Brett, were perfectly proper, and in Orr's best interests. Alluding to the core of Orr's discontent—that no job had been found—Panzee repeated his belief that FCUSA must not try to influence academic appointments and that following settlement Orr could be restored to academic life: 'Mere shouting at large cannot do so: it is no substitute for courage in facing the matter in one's own university'.[267]

Three days later all staff associations received a telegram from Brian Medlin of Adelaide University, stating: 'Orr solicitor's state Wright's memo contains grossly erroneous statements, inferences and impressions seriously detrimental to Orr's interests.' He followed up with a lengthy letter claiming Orr to have been 'put in an almost impossible position'.[268] That really did make Panzee growl. On 9 February he informed Champion that he would no longer act as Orr's 'next friend' since Orr had 'done a Kerr Wootten on me'. He tried one more time to impress upon the enthusiastic lawyer that the 'new evidence' was not up to much. 'It is overly optimistic to think this will clear Orr—it could boomerang.' He gave a final warning: 'if he does not accept these terms and insists on running around with fools like Medlin and going into court to get the can emptied over him, he will know what devastation is.'[269]

The special meeting of FCUSA held at the University of New South Wales on 14 February was lengthy and painful. Orr had sought leave to appear, as had Ginnane. Both were heard. Orr was given five minutes which he considerably extended in an emotional address, distributing as well a twenty-two page document outlining his case and attacking Panzee for making agreements on his behalf. Desperate to stop FCUSA making a settlement with the university, he pleaded: 'Why should I be forced, under the threat of removal of moral and academic support by my colleagues at a time when there is additional new evidence of an unusual kind supporting my innocence.' If they were to agree to settlement, he concluded, they would be 'dispensing with moral and academic principles and requirements of justice'. His plea in person was more succinct: 'here I am asked to give up the fight to vindicate myself, to clear my name, with nothing in return for it.'

Ginnane also told the meeting that the only possible just restitution for Orr would be his reinstatement and full compensation for ten years lost salary. Brett was firm in rejecting these appeals: 'We cannot ask Tasmania to do any more than it has done,' he said. In essence the terms could be no more than those agreed in 1963. The overwhelming majority of the delegates supported Brett to lift the censure.[270]

Orr's reaction was vitriolic. To the hapless Stout, under pressure to effect the same agreement on behalf of the philosophers, he wrote nine pages of diatribe attacking almost everyone, even Ginnane, but none more than 'Professor Wright', as he now referred to Panzee, who was 'now apparently quite ruthless bent on misrepresenting [me] in order to make me party to the abandonment of principle'.[271] Poor Stout was really depressed by this fallout between close allies, but helpless to do anything about it. Panzee was not a man to change his course once he had decided it; and he had decided to be done with Orr, as he told Sadie Orr on 25 February; he was abandoning her husband to his lawyers—'I am not and will not be associated with him again.'[272]

Could it be that after all those years of aiding and abetting Orr in his persistent character assassinations; after watching the pool of villains grow ever wider; could it be that Panzee was actually surprised to have Orr turn on him as well? He was not a man for irony, so he would not have in any way appreciated that it was to the patronised and abused Stout that Orr unleashed his vitriol about Panzee and the 'abandonment of principle'. Stout, who had never made the wholehearted commitment to Orr that Panzee had, was well aware of Orr's two-facedness and took it in his stride. When he received a glowing letter of appreciation from Orr he noted with some wry amusement that this contrasted 'in an extraordinary way with the letter he wrote to Sandy Anderson attacking me violently'.[273] To Panzee, suggestions of Orr's duplicity had always seemed like scurrilous defamations. Yet he of all people should have understood, from almost daily exposure, that Orr's actions were always and entirely self-interested. Only those people, pitifully few, who were prepared to serve his interests unreservedly were spared the sting of Orr's vituperation. As Edwin Tanner observed of Orr, his behaviour resembled that of 'a half rational ant, unpredictable elusive, wanting, wanting, and ever ready to sting those who would not give'.[274] Nevertheless, Panzee was special. He had been tireless in his proselytising and his detective work. He had contributed over £10 000 in the support of Orr's family. He had nailed his not-inconsiderable reputation to Orr's mast. The Orr case was his case too. I can't help feeling for his profound disappointment. Panzee had a blind spot when it came to Sydney Sparkes Orr: he wanted to see him as a heroic Celtic champion of just causes, never as the flawed and deluded man that he was. I am sure I don't know why Panzee persisted with his view of Orr as being on the side of the angels (or mythic

Celtic heroes) in the face of such damaging evidence to the contrary. He didn't even like the man; thought him a twit, or so he said, in retrospect, some thirty years later.

Was he bitterly hurt? If he was he kept it very much to himself. His wife told me she was unaware of the schism between her husband and Orr, but agreed the greater the hurt the more likely he was to be silent. Significantly she drew my attention to the obituary for Panzee where Davis McGaughey reported that when asked 'What makes you angry?' Panzee had replied 'When someone is guilefully treacherous.' Mmmm.

Orr did not have his day in court. On his lawyers' advice he signed the deed of settlement in hospital in early April; the details were released to the media on 6 May. Soon after he was readmitted to hospital, gravely ill. Knowing he was dying, he called his old colleague Sam Warren Carey, president of the staff association, to his bedside, to talk about providing support for his wife, Sadie. He made one last effort to convince Carey that he had never been intimate with Suzanne Kemp. Gently Carey deflected him from this purpose. There was no point, Carey told Orr, he was 'completely convinced' that Suzanne had been telling the truth. 'Orr did not press the matter, because he knew that I knew.'[275]

CHAPTER TEN

Terrible hurt was done to a lot of people

In his rather coy account of the Orr case, the University of Tasmania's official historian, Richard Davis, remarks that the case 'had many of the elements of Greek tragedy'.[276] Certainly Sydney Sparkes Orr was a classic case of hubris: his overweening sense of his own uniqueness, his almost messianic belief in the redemptive power of his hedonism, his utter self-absorption, all led him with seeming inevitability to disgrace and premature death. He was not the only one. A whiff of hubris clings to Panzee Wright, whose crusade to expose the inherent venality of the Tasmanian ruling class he so despised, blinded him to manipulations and delusions of 'poor old Syd'; but Panzee was a big man for whom the Orr case, however compelling, was just one item in a life of public controversy. It did him no harm, over the long haul. There was really only one man, other than the deluded Orr, for whom the affair might be said to be a nemesis: Sir John Morris, the chancellor castigated by the royal commission in 1955. Appointed chancellor in 1944 when he was an extremely youthful chief justice, Morris applied his energy and will to building the decrepit institution into a genuine university. Fair-minded and a vigorous champion of the academy, Morris was however notoriously arbitrary, authoritarian and egotistic, perceiving his position in very proactive terms. He largely usurped the role of the part-time vice-chancellor, Morris Miller, and reduced Miller's full-time successor, Torleiv Hytten, to little more than a cipher. As Sam Warren Carey observed of Morris, whom he admired and regarded as a friend, he needed to play the role of Caesar. Opposition was not tolerated, least of all if it came from professors, whom Morris took to be the employees of his council. On his own volition he had the standards of matriculation dropped, which had the happy consequence of permitting his son entry to the university. Cries of nepotism did not faze him. 'Let them hurl their slanders,' he told Carey, 'My shoulders are broad.'[277] Still, he demanded that the resolution of the professorial board opposing his move be deleted from the minutes. That was the measure of the man. With much the same sureness he had determined that Sydney Sparkes Orr be appointed to the foundation chair of philosophy.

Morris knew what he wanted; and what he didn't want. He didn't want any moral relativists or atheistic doubters, and he didn't want any scholarly aesthetes either. Paul Grice, then a very promising senior fellow of St John's College Oxford, had let it be known he would welcome an invitation to the chair at Hobart. He had Buckley's. Morris wasn't so much interested in scholarship. He wanted a sound Christian fellow who could speak out against communism and take a stand on moral issues in the community—a Malcolm Muggeridge sort of chap. Before the chair was advertised he had some intimations about who could fit the bill.

Both Morris and Hytten had received an unsolicited letter from Sir Frederick Eggleston on that very subject. In January 1951, the old man of Australian liberalism wrote to say that he knew someone 'who is qualified to fill the chair as no-one else in Australia,' although, 'that is not my main reason for writing.' His real concern was to have the chair filled by a philosopher 'capable of displaying some qualities of intellectual leadership in these critical times'. Eggleston believed there was a conspiracy to fill all the chairs of philosophy with men who had turned the weighty moral concerns of philosophy into 'mere logical techniques'. The leader of this school of thought, in which Eggleston included not just logical positivists but any kind of linguistic analysis, was Gilbert Ryle at Oxford, who, according to Eggleston 'has sworn that he will not be satisfied until all the chairs in the empire are filled by men of this school ... arid, relativist and neutral on all great moral and intellectual issues'. (Maybe this is why Ryle came to refer to the University of Tasmania as 'that looney bin'.)

When philosophers eschew their concern with great moral issues they create an intellectual vacuum which is 'filled by irrational activist movements like communism', Eggleston solemnly warned his correspondents. In his biography *of* Eggleston, Warren Osmond writes of Eggleston's alienation from the dominant trends of postwar philosophy, which he did not understand and which he profoundly distrusted. He had not read Wittgenstein. His concern about Ryle caused him to actively intervene in the selection for the chair of social philosophy at ANU: Karl Popper, the favoured candidate, was rejected because Eggleston feared that he was tainted by logical positivism.

In a hand-written note, Eggleston confided to Hytten, whom he knew well, that the man he had in mind was Sydney Sparkes Orr. 'I am not qualified to judge his philosophical standing, but I can speak for his honesty and courage.' No doubt Eggleston had been alerted to the prospect of the chair by Orr, whom he knew through involvement in adult education and the Student Christian Movement. They had exchanged views on Eggleston's latest project, a book on the philosophical basis of the social sciences. He would have known from Orr that there were serious tensions between Orr and his professor, Boyce Gibson. Eggleston was free with his advice in that quarter also, pointing out that Gibson was captive to the positivists in his department and 'lacks the guts to assert himself'. Moreover, he understood that Gibson would back his brother Quentin for the chair. Quentin Gibson, who defended a positivist view of the social sciences, had written 'nothing so far of any value', Eggleston asserted.[278]

These opinions from the esteemed Eggleston were warmly appreciated by the recipients, with Hytten reassuring Eggleston that he and Morris were 'naturally not keen to get a man of the Ryle school' and that they would 'give due weight to your recommendation, which, as you know, I personally value very much.'[279] So much did he value it that Hytten kept Eggleston informed on who had applied and what had been said about them; all of which Eggleston promised 'to keep confidential from Orr'. These unofficial briefings gave Eggleston the opportunity to bag the other candidates, especially the most impressive, John Mackie. 'Have you read Mackie's paper on the refutation of morality? It is a typical example of the superficial way in which present day students dispose of questions of such importance,' he wrote. By contrast, the philosophical basis of morality 'is a question on which Orr has done much work', or that is what he had been told.[280]

Eggleston's views on what represented a sound philosophical approach were echoed by another old man with a desire to cast the future to his liking. Morris Miller, having retired as vice-chancellor in 1944, remained professor of psychology and philosophy until 1951, when, aged seventy, he finally retired. It was as a result of his finally leaving that a separate chair was to be created. Another pre-Wittgenstein man, Miller also looked on Orr with enthusiasm, for much the same reasons as Eggleston. To their recommendations the chancellor could add another unsolicited booster from adult educator, Derek van Abbe, who felt Morris should consider Orr, 'a real Christian and a scholar' adding 'incidentally' that he was a 'very keen adult educator'.[281] Morris' great enthusiasm for adult education as a bulwark against communism and moral decay was well known. Sydney Orr looked like the chancellor's man.

The chair was decided by a committee of five, chaired by Morris, including no external professorial members and no philosophers. It is a matter of common knowledge that Morris insisted on Orr's appointment, supported by Hytten and Miller. The representatives of the professorial board and council strongly disagreed. They accepted confidential opinion tendered from philosophers (including Alan Stout) that all three other candidates, Kurt Baier, Quentin Gibson and John Mackie, were superior to Orr. Hastening to tell Eggleston of Orr's success, Hytten allowed that the committee found the decision difficult, but 'your recommendation certainly helped.'[282] The academic world was appalled. Philosophers tell me that at the height of his distinguished career Paul Grice was still bitter that he had been ignored in favour of a nobody like Orr.

One of the most persistent stories about Orr is that he got his job thanks to glowing references from Boyce Gibson, who wanted to get rid of him from Melbourne. Certainly this was the story Hytten liked to tell, once Orr had become a gross embarrassment to him. It is not true. Orr got glowing references from no one. In his application he included references from distinguished scholars in England, such as Lindsay Keir, who admitted he had no knowledge of Orr since the time he was a student who showed promise at Queen's. His colleagues from Melbourne offered faint praise, stressing his zeal and enthusiasm to bring philosophy to the layman in his adult education classes. Gibson gave an uncritical, but not fulsome, reference. It is what Boyce Gibson said in his confidential report to the selection committee which really tells the story. Classing the four applicants in descending order, he placed Orr 'well below' the others, and felt constrained to say that Orr could not work with those who did not agree with him, students or colleagues, and that he was deficient in both discretion and dignity.[283] Unequivocal comment, don't you think?

By the time these unwelcome opinions had reached the chancellor he had already made up his mind. Caesar was going to have his Christian moralist even if the philosophers thought little of him. Had not Eggleston warned him to expect tainted views from Boyce Gibson?

It didn't take Sir John Morris long to realise what academics were already saying: that the appointment of Orr 'was his own ghastly blunder'.[284] He was chairing a prestigious public meeting with Julian Huxley as guest speaker when the newly arrived professor of philosophy took everyone by surprise by launching into an extended and far from coherent tirade. Obviously discomfited, Morris tried several times, without success, to get Orr to ask a question or sit down. 'If he could, he would have got down off the stage and throttled him,' one onlooker gleefully remembers.[285] In the university staffroom Morris' blunder was apparent almost at once. Ken Dallas says Orr evoked derisive laughter when he told them that the chancellor expected him to make pronouncements on important public issues. 'Orr showed no resentment at the laughter; his self-centred smugness could have received it as approval.'[286] Orr did not appreciate how inappropriate his first attempt to put Morris' edict to work had been. It was with much self-satisfaction that he told Edwin Tanner how he had upset the great Julian Huxley by challenging the theory of evolution.

Orr's most spectacular opportunity to play the role for which he had been anointed came when he wrote his immoderate public letter to the premier on the parlous state of Morris' university, and demanded a royal commission. The upshot of that impetuous move was that his patron was publicly humiliated and castigated for exactly the kind of paternalistic intervention in academic affairs which had secured the professor of philosophy his job. Reflecting on Orr's stupidity, Dallas observes that 'on his own say so', Orr set himself up as 'a rebel against the poobah who had selected him'. Morris took it hard; both Orr's treachery, as he saw it, and the commission finding. Hytten believed the royal commission largely contributed to Morris' sudden and premature death the following year. Dallas, less charitable, suggests Morris 'died of shame when he realized he was a failure. His poobah role in a small state was beyond his power; yet he saw himself as infallible.' So too, Dallas concluded, Orr died one decade later when he was forced to realise that his estimate of his own worth was misplaced—an ironic echo of the man who had chosen him.[287]

Many people think that the University of Tasmania brought trauma and international disgrace down upon its own head by the improper dismissal of Professor Orr in 1956. I do not agree that the university should have to wear that ignominy. But I do think the university administration was derelict in the process of Orr's appointment. The appointment of a professor, especially to a foundation chair, has always been a highly politicised process, and in the 1950s the chairs of philosophy were seen to be strategic in the way sociology chairs were seen to be in the 1970s; but the enormous influence of the chancellor and the outgoing professor in Orr's appointment, the intervention of powerful external forces beyond the discipline putting non-academic considerations of politics and religion above philosophical qualifications, together with the deliberate exclusion of an external member with philosophical credentials were quite improper. Discussion of the Orr case has focused completely on the question of proper procedures for the dismissal of professors, but it might be an idea to shift the focus to proper procedures for the appointment of professors. Had these been followed in 1952, there would never have been an Orr case, at least not one which involved the University of Tasmania. It may be that Orr turned out to be much more unhinged than anyone could have predicted; but if the Orr case is to be regarded as an exemplar of academic principle, a case study in academic procedures, then the issue of whether he was properly appointed is indissoluble from the issue of whether or not he was properly dismissed. You reap what you sow, we are told—something Hytten conveniently overlooked when he lashed out at the University of Melbourne for passing him off with a lemon.

On the face of it, the international ban on Orr's vacant chair did suggest that the philosophy fraternity believed that having blundered in appointing Orr the university should have to live with it, regardless of academic and personal trauma. But in actuality no one, except maybe Bill Ginnane, believed Orr must be reinstated at Tasmania. Alan Stout, president of the

Association of Philosophers, was quite clear about this when he approached the university for a new inquiry in 1958 (even though he couldn't resist the dig 'You would never have got him in the first place if you had taken the best advice—including mine'). To prospective applicants Stout was reassuringly confident that the chair would be legitimately open, in the near future, Orr having secured his just deserts and gone elsewhere. The Association of Philosophers simply wanted the matter of Orr's misconduct established, or otherwise, to their satisfaction. It might well have been, to quote Stout again, that Orr 'was guilty as hell', in which case he could expect to get nothing.[288] Yet it is curious that Professor Stout was prepared to lend credence to the suggestion that the young woman who made the complaint against Orr was an hysterical dissembler; an accomplished liar who manufactured evidence and connived with others to defraud the court; curious also that he, who had little time for the intellectual processes of the church, should privilege the finding of an ecclesiastical court over that of the High Court in the matter of Suzanne's veracity. Since Stout maintained an impeccably neutral position ('I do not know whether or not the alleged sexual relation took place'), I wonder why was he so prejudiced toward Suzanne as to write:

> elaborate fabrications of non-existent sexual adventures are not unknown, especially when the fabricator is passing through a period of 'turbulent eroticism' (to quote the High Court judgement), and such inventions could be sparked off by the rejection of her advances ('Hell hath no fury ...') And as her 'diary' shows, Miss Kemp had the power of creative imagination to invent such stories and perhaps come to believe them.[289]

I also wonder why, since he claimed not to know, he was so sure 'it is nonsense to talk about Orr using his position to seduce or break down the resistance of Miss Kemp.' Was it because he was aware, as one could scarcely fail to be aware at university, that some impressionable young women were eager to establish a relationship with their lecturers, just as Suzanne had been eager. Surely he was not so otherworldly that he failed to notice the occasions where student infatuations flowered into sexual liaisons; in his own university, in his own department. Was it only when a student made a complaint that they could be said to be indulging in 'elaborate fabrications'? No other female students in a sexual relationship had found it a matter for complaint, had they?

Likewise the executive members of FCUSA were adamant they had no intention 'to coerce the university willy nilly into taking Professor Orr back'.[290] No, they wanted merely to establish to their satisfaction, using procedures they approved, whether or not Orr was guilty of misconduct. On that matter their minds were admirably open. If he were guilty, then he deserved to be sacked, they said. What particularly exercised their indignation was the nature of the proof required. It was not proved 'beyond all reasonable doubt' that Orr had seduced Suzanne Kemp. He was sacked on evidence that 'would not hang a dog', they insisted, wilfully understating the persuasive evidence that was given to support Suzanne's story. FCUSA demanded the standard of proof reserved for criminal offence because they believed the penalty for Orr was so grave (and sexual accusations so notoriously difficult to prove). A man's whole career was at stake on the word of a girl student. No matter what poor opinion they might have of Orr, personally, and largely the opinion was very poor, his dismissal could not be permitted to set a precedent for professors being undone on the say-so of a student.

That is how the issue looked to the members of the staff association at the University of Tasmania who tried repeatedly to dissuade their mainland colleagues from running on the Orr case. As Roy Chappell pointed out to one prestigious academic wishing to beat the drum for Orr: 'Talk of academic freedom is easy to convert cynically into talk of academic license.'[291]

Why else so coolly pass over well-substantiated allegations of harassment of colleagues? Why else pointedly disregard proof that Orr lied about his qualifications? Why else suppress evidence that Orr had a previous history of sexual impropriety? These matters were deemed to be 'irrelevant' to the critical issue. And the critical issue was to show that Suzanne could not prove 'beyond all reasonable doubt' that she had been sexually intimate with her professor. It was her word against his. FCUSA was clear about that. But what this was signalling was that the word of the academic carried more weight than the word of the student in such matters. After all, he had so much to lose.

This was the early 1960s, when academics were almost exclusively male and where it was cultural practice to dress up male privilege in the garb of principle. As FCUSA secretary Ken Buckley acknowledged later, 'sexual harassment was not on the agenda.'[292] Too right it wasn't. Nor did it get on the agenda for a long time. Suzanne Kemp was at the centre of the first sexual harassment case in university history, maybe in Australian history. An in-house inquiry and two court judgements upheld her claims that Professor Orr had used his position to persuade her into an adulterous sexual liaison. In prestigious academic circles she was branded hysteric, liar, psychopathic bitch, easy lay, while Professor Orr was hailed as Australia's Dreyfus. The university which dismissed Orr, as the professional academic organisations agreed was appropriate if the allegations were true, was subjected to eight years of censure and bans. Small wonder that sexual harassment as an issue between staff and students still tends to be off the agenda on most campuses.

Students have found ways to lodge complaints less damaging than Suzanne Kemp's. At Sydney University in the mid-1970s a rash of graffiti began appearing in the women's toilets making negative sexual assessments of a number of libertine male academics. You know what I mean: *Dr Bloggs is a lousy fuck* or *Associate Professor Nerd has crabs.* The men who were the object of these cryptic messages, at least those I knew, were outraged, and deeply suspicious. It was obviously some feminist piece of character assassination, since none of the students with whom they had been intimate could possibly have reason to seek retribution. I thought it was very funny; both their offended sensibilities and the messages. I also appreciated that the joke signalled a changing perception about sexual politics on campus, with students beginning to feel that the exploitation of an unequal power relationship should attract penalty and public disclosure. It did not mean that students showed less of the wide-eyed infatuation which made them easy (some said irresistible) conquests. Such is the nature of the university for many young people—and older people too—when whole new ways of experiencing the world begin to open up for them. Those who are seen to have privileged access to this intoxicating realm of ideas are often perceived as having an allure far in excess of their real endowments. One of the things I find particularly silly about the Orr defence is the notion that Suzanne could not possibly have been seduced by Orr because he was so unattractive. Students are impressionable. They are vulnerable. The confused and intoxicated girl revealed in Suzanne Kemp's diary is instantly recognisable to anyone who has spent time in universities, and to those who have been students themselves. Academics have a special duty toward their students, just as psychiatrists have toward their patients, to recognise the power their situation has invested in them and exercise extreme care in their personal interactions with students. That much is understood in codes of conduct for academics. How much it is understood in practice is a matter for cynical speculation.

My defence of the dismissal of Orr invariably triggers indignant cries that I think academics should be sacked for having affairs with their students. Well, I don't think that. But neither do I think that sexual relationships between academics and students always merit the benign appellation of 'affair'. In such an unequal power relationship, questions of volition are not straightforward. Issues of coercion and harassment, implicit or explicit, need to be considered, as they were considered, meticulously, by Justice Green in the Orr case. I am not aware of any sexual harassment cases which have been brought against academics recently, where anyone has been sacked, or that it has been seriously suggested such a strong penalty should apply. But in the Orr case, thirty-five years ago, it was almost universally accepted, and reiterated by professional organisations, that an academic who seduced a student should be dismissed. He did. He was. If his academic supporters thought that such a penalty was unreasonable they should have publicly said so, instead of making slurs on Suzanne Kemp's character and credibility.

No one would deny that the costs to Orr were considerable, and to his family just as great. It was not Orr, but his wife, Sadie, who had to plead for money from the staff associations and face the humiliation of accounting to them for every penny in her household budget. But it was Orr himself who prolonged the whole pitiful business. As his contemporaries noted, Orr liked his role. He found a focus for his libidinal energy and an importance he would otherwise have only dreamed of. Wanting to be a martyr, he became one. He cast himself as the centrepiece in a vast and sinister conspiracy of such importance that he felt it necessary to speak of himself in the third person. 'I think he could have gone on indefinitely,' James McAuley observed. 'He had enormous powers, it was his career. He made a second career out of the Orr case.'[293]

McAuley also attests that 'terrible hurt was done to a lot of people;' people on the periphery like Carey, Townsley, Wootten and McAuley were profoundly affected. 'I have never quite recovered,' McAuley said, echoing a common sentiment. Dr Milanov and his traumatised wife had their dream of a tranquil new life utterly destroyed. Mrs Isles watched her husband's health deteriorate rapidly during the case and saw him retire early as a semi-invalid, his high hopes for the university crushed under the contempt of academic associations. Others have said that the strain of the case affected the health and well-being of Orr's supporters Harry Eddy and Malcolm McCrae. Friendships were broken irrevocably; families split into hostile camps. The cost to Edwin Tanner was enormous. It blighted his life. Writing about it in 1966 made him feel sick. He persisted because 'there are two men on trial here. I stood to gain nothing but ignominy ... I expected expulsion. I was sad for Orr, his family and my family. I was sad for myself.' The other student who complained, Suzanne Kemp, a vulnerable young woman, had her intimate sexual experiences and naive indiscretions splashed over the nation's newspapers. Since then she has had to endure decades of slander and scurrilous rumour. Her motives and credibility have been the subject of infamous slurs. I do not imagine she will welcome this book. For reasons I entirely understand, she declined to talk to me. I do know that she attempted to resume her university studies in 1975, only to find that she was subject to a ban by the student union, said to apply to every campus. It is not possible for the student union to actually stop someone from enrolling at a university, but Suzanne, a brilliant student, did not resume her studies that year, nor has she any year since.

I believe these two students were very courageous to make a complaint against their professor. They took enormous risks with their own futures over what they saw to be a matter of principle: the abuse of academic privilege. In the great matter of principle which so absorbed the academic associations, when they took up the Orr case, the witness of these students has persistently been devalued and discredited.

I should not be surprised if the Kemp family came to bitterly regret having made a complaint against Orr. I am sure that Dr Milanov did. But Edwin Tanner said that if he were to encounter the same situation he would respond in same way, without his idealism: 'having lived through those experiences, and my experience with Professor Wright, I would expect, in future, no more decency from professors than from any other grown and educated man.'[294]

BIBLIOGRAPHY

Manuscript sources

High Court Appeal Book 1957, R Eggleston papers, Melbourne University archives

RD Wright papers, Melbourne University archives

AK Stout papers, Sydney University archives

KI Isles papers, University of Tasmania archives

University of Tasmania Staff Association papers, University of Tasmania archives

K Dallas papers, University of Tasmania archives

The Orr case papers, University of Tasmania archives

FCUSA/FAUSA papers, Australian National University department of business and labour archives

Australian Council for Cultural Freedom papers, Australian National Library

J Latham papers, Australian National Library

F Eggleston papers, Australian National Library

D Horne papers, Mitchell Library

G Harwood papers, Fryer Library, University of Queensland

N Rawling collection, ANU department of business and labour archives

J Passmore papers, Australian National Library

M Diesendorf papers, Australian Defence Forces Academy archives Tasmanian Supreme Court records, State Library of Tasmania archives Presbyterian Church of Tasmania records, State Library of Tasmania archives

Unpublished memoirs

S Warren Carey, University of Tasmania archives

T Hytten, University of Tasmania archives

E Tanner, private

P Berry, private

K Dallas, University of Tasmania archives

Taped interviews

RD Wright interviewed by J Power, University of Melbourne

J McAuley interviewed by C Santamaria, Australian National Library

E Barber, M Hills, J Polya, K Dallas, AK Stout, J Cardno, University of Tasmania centenary series, University of Tasmania archives

Personal interviews by author

M Ambrose, Hobart, November 1991

AS, Melbourne, July 1991

P Berry, Hobart, October 1991

T Bowden, Sydney, December 1991

K Buckley, Sydney, November 1991

C Christensen, Melbourne, November 1991

S Warren Carey, Hobart, August 1991

J Clarke, Hobart, October 1991

J Coleman, Hobart, August 1991

P Cranswick, Hobart, October 1991

H Findlay, Hobart, November 1991

G Firth, Hobart, August 1991

B Ginnane, Canberra, February 1992

G Harrison, Hobart, December 1991

A Hoddinott, Sydney, July 1991

W Hodgman, Hobart, November 1991

D Horne, Sydney, November 1991

Mrs K Isles, Hobart, November 1991

R Jennings, Hobart, June 1992

B Joske, Hobart, June 1992

T Kearney, Hobart, August 1991

P Lake, Hobart, March 1992

J Locher, Hobart, March 1992

Mrs E Wojtowicz, Hobart, August 1991

WN Oats, Hobart, May 1992

S Porteous, Hobart, May 1991

M Roe, Hobart, June 1992

R Rothfield, Melbourne, July 1991

G Scrivener, Hobart, May 1992

V and S Smith, Sydney, November 1991

R Solomon, Sydney, November 1991

S and J Tanner, Melbourne, May 1992

S Thomas, Hobart, August 1991

WA Townsley, Hobart, May 1991

T Wheelwright, Sydney, November 1991

H Wootten, Sydney, February 1992

Lady M Wright, Melbourne, February 1992

Printed sources

'Assassins in Hobart', *Nation*, 13 February 1960

Australian Association of Philosophers, *Report to the AAP Council on the Moves for a Settlement of the Orr Case*, Sydney, 1964

Allen, HC 'Australian Causes', *New Statesman*, 26 January 1962

Anderson, J 'The Orr Case and Academic Freedom', *Observer*, 28 June 1958

Bartos, M 'The Academic Freedom Charter', *Australian Universities Review* 33, 1&2, 1990

Boyce, P 'What Price Justice?', *Crux*, September 1963

Coleman, P 'Slamming the Door', *Bulletin*, 26 August 1961

Davis, R *Open to Talent: the University of Tasmania 1890–1990*, University of Tasmania, Hobart, 1990

'Free Academics or Council Servants: Tasmania University Staff before the Murray Report', *Vestes* 2, 1985

The Royal Commission and the Orr Case, unpublished paper, Hobart, 1989

Dorset, A 'Orr's First Five Years', *Bulletin*, 1 February 1961

Eddy, WCH 'Some Reflections on the Orr Case', *Australian Highway* 40, 2, 1959

Eddy, WCH Orr, Jacaranda, Brisbane, 1961

Eddy, WCH 'Professor Sydney Sparkes Orr', *Vestes*, September 1966

Fitzpatrick, B 'An Injustice Has Been Done', *Meanjin*, April 1961

Ginnane, W 'Orr: Institutional Corruption and the Tired Conscience', *Prospect* 3, 1961

'Reinstating Orr', *Prospect* 5, 1962

'Orr—The Inevitable Settlement', *Bulletin* 28 December 1963

Hall, R 'Dropping the Albatross', *Bulletin*, 28 December 1963

Horne, Donald, 'Sidetracking the Orr case', *Observer*, 18 October 1958

'Orr, Kerr and Wootten', *Observer*, 1 November 1958

'Orr Kerr and Wootten II', *Observer*, 15 November 1958

'No end of the Affair', *Bulletin*, 2 September 1961

'A Grave Offense Against Public Morality', *Bulletin*, 23 September 1961

Isles, K *The Dismissal of SS Orr by the University of Tasmania*, University of Tasmania, Hobart, 1958

Kerr J, & Wootten, H 'Re-Opening the Orr Case', *Free Spirit*, August 1958

'A Rejoinder', *Free Spirit*, September/October 1958

Kerr, J 'Academic Freedom and Academic Boycott', *Australian Quarterly* 30, 4, 1958

Martin, B, Baker, CMA, Manwell, C and Pugh, C (eds), *Intellectual Suppression: Australian Case Histories, Analysis and Responses*, Angus & Robertson, Sydney, 1986

McGregor, C 'Orr for the Mainland', *Nation*, 22 August 1964

Molnar, G 'Sexual Freedom in the Orr Case', *Australian Highway*, June 1960

Montrose, J 'Orr', *Universities Quarterly*, February 1962

Orr, SS 'The Professor's Strange Love Story' (six parts), *Pix*, 1 June—20 July 1957

The Orr Case: A Critical Examination of the Procedure, Evidence and Judgement, roneoed, Hobart, 1957

'The Struggle for Justice and the Preservation of a Heritage', *Diogenes*, September 1961

Osmond, W Frederick Eggleston: *An Intellectual in Australian Politics*, Allen & Unwin, Sydney, 1985

Pavkovik, A (ed) *Contemporary Yugoslav Philosophy*, Nijhof International Philosophy series, Amsterdam, 1988

Polya, JB 'The University of Tasmania: Scandal or Tragedy', *Vestes*, 5, 1, 1962

Polyani, G 'University Crisis in Tasmania', *Science and Freedom* 4, 1955

Report of the Royal Commission into the University of Tasmania, Tasmanian Government Printer, Hobart, 1955

Rish, B The Tasmanian University Union 1899–1972, BA(Hons) thesis, University of Tasmania, 1981

Scots Kirk Session, 'Formal Finding and Observations on the Fama Clamosa Anent Professor Sydney Sparkes Orr', Hobart, 1958

Stout AK 'The Academic Point of View', *Free Spirit* 4, 10 August, 1958

'The Orr Case', *Arna*, 1958

'The Orr trials and Miss Kemp's Diary', *Observer* 9, June 1958

'The Philosophers and the Orr Case', *Australian Quarterly* 31, 1, 1959

'The Staff Association and the Orr Case', *Vestes* 2, 1, 1959

'Tasmania Virulent', *Nation*, 28 January 1961

Thorpe, RH, and Buckley, K 'Report on a Visit to the Tasmanian Association', *Vestes* 1,5, 1958

Turner, I 'The Orr Case', *Overland*, August 1961

Wootten, JH 'The Orr Dismissal and the Universities', *Quadrant* 1, 2, 1957

Wright, RD 'The Orr Case: Against Special Pleading', *Observer*, 15 November 1958

The Orr Case: Narrative and Abstractions, roneoed, Melbourne, 1958

'A Reply to JR Kerr QC & JH Wootten', *Free Spirit*, September/October 1958

'Lawyers and Justice', *Observer*, 23 August 1958

LIST OF ABBREVIATIONS

ADFA
Australian Defence Forces Academy Library

AKS
Alan Ker Stout papers, University of Sydney archives

ANL
Australian National Library

ANUBL
Australian National University department of business and labor

RDW
Roy Douglas Wright papers, Melbourne University archives

RE
Richard Eggleston papers, Melbourne University archives

SLTA
State Library of Tasmania Archives

UQFL
University of Queensland Fryer Library

UT
University of Tasmania archives

UTSA
University of Tasmania Staff Association papers

NOTES

Chapter 1

1 · Carey memoir

2 · All references to Suzanne Kemp's letters, diary, and testimony are drawn from the Appeal Book compiled for the High Court in 1957, RE

Chapter 2

3 · John Anderson, 'The Orr Case and Academic Freedom', *Observer*, 28 June 1958

4 · George Molnar, 'Sexual Freedom in the Orr Case', *Australian Highway*, June 1960

5 · Australian Association of Philosophers, *Report to the AAP Council on Moves For a Settlement of the Orr Case*, Sydney, 1964

6 · WHC Eddy, 'Professor Sydney Sparkes Orr', *Vestes* 9, 3, 1966

Chapter 3

7 · The correspondence concerning Orr's academic career at St Andrews is to be found in RDW 1/1/7

8 · Macbeath to Stout, 3 March 1960, AKS 740

9 · Ernest Davey to James Irvine, 16 October 1945, RDW 1/1/7

10 · Jonathon Tate to James Irvine, 21 May 1945, RDW 1/1/7

11 · Dr Annette Smith to author, February 1992

12 · Smith to author, February 1992; Robert Smart to author, December 1991

13 · Joske interview

14 · Caldicott to author, 29 September 1991

15 · Grover to author, 11 March 1992

16 · Gasking to Stout, nd May 1958, AKS 716

17 · Gibson's references can be found at RDW 1/1/18

18 · R Sussex to author, 2 December 1991

19 · M Sussex to author, 2 December 1991

20 · AS to Bishop Cranswick, June 1953, RDW 1/1/10; AS interview

21 · Cranswick to Hytten, 30 May 1956, UT 47/126

22 · Supreme Court transcript, RE

23 · Milanov to Carrington, 18 May 1954; Carrington to Milanov, 21 May 1954, RDW 1/1/22

24 · Orr to Hytten, 7 June 1954, RDW 1/1/7

25 · *Report of the Royal Commission into the University of Tasmania*, 1955, UT C8

26 · Chappell papers, UTSA C9

27 · Hytten memoir, UT 127

28 · Dallas memoir, UT 516

29 · Townsley interview; Supreme Court transcript, RE

30 · Polya to Chappell, 5 December 1956, UTSA Cl2

31 · Orr submission, RDW 1/1/2

32 · Tanner memoir

33 · Polya taped interview, UT 388

34 · Ambrose interview

35 · Tanner memoir

36 · Bowden interview

37 · Ambrose interview

38 · Tanner memoir

39 · Locher interview; Lake interview; student testimonials, RDW 1/2/3

40 · Tanner memoir

41 · Jan Tanner interview

42 · Dallas to Higgins, 29 May 1957, Norman Rawling collection, ANUBL, N 57/181

43 · Carey memoir

44 · Milanov to Hytten, 2 May 1955, UT 47/126

45 · Hytten memoir, UT 127

46 · Hytten, Supreme Court transcript RE

47 · Cranswick statement, 30 May 1956, UT 47/126

48 · Tanner to Hytten, 2 December 1955, UT 47/126

49 · Tanner to Diesendorf, 29 September 1976, Margaret Diesendorf papers, ADFA

50 · Tanner memoir; Supreme Court transcript RE

51 · Orr to Hytten, 8 December 1955, UT 47 /126

52 · Tanner memoir

53 · Orr to Toulmin, 17 August 1956, AKS 485

54 · Morris to Latham, 27 March 1956, Latham papers, ANL 1009/71

55 · Firth interview

56 · Gow to Hytten 19 December 1955, UT 47/126

57 · Harrison interview

Chapter 4

58 · Oats interview

59 · Hytten memoir, UT 127

60 · Harrison interview

61 · Polya to Chappell, 5 December 1956, UTSA C12

62 · Harrison interview

63 · Morris to Latham, 27 March 1956, Latham papers, ANL

1009/71/326

64 · Quoted in Eddy, *Orr*, p 261.

65 · Morris to Latham, 27 March 1956, Latham papers, ANL 1009/71/326

66 · Firth to Dallas, 30 May 1956, 26 June 1956, UT 516

67 · Dallas memoir, UT 516

68 · Orr, *Mercury*, 27 May 1957

69 · FCUSA Inquiry into the Orr case, February 1961, UTSA C10

70 · TG Room, letter to the Adelaide *Advertiser*, August 1958

71 · D Horne, *Bulletin*, 23 September 1961

72 · Orr, The Orr case: A Critical Examination of the Procedure, Evidence and Judgement, nd November 1957, RDW 1/1/6

73 · Morris Miller, draft statement, 12 June 1956, UTSA C10

74 · Stout, *Free Spirit*, 23 March 1956

75 · Wright, The Orr Case: Narrative and Abstractions, 1958, AKS 716

76 · Sawyer to McCrae, UTSA C10

77 · Chappell to Polyani, 17 December 1956, UTSA C12

78 · Todd to SS Orr, 19 November 1957, UTSA C9

79 · McManners, 15 July 1958, AKS 485

80 · Orr, *Age*, 20 June 1958

81 · Chappell, UTSA C12

82 · Lake interview

83 · Polya and Cardno taped interviews, UT 388

Chapter 5

84 · Papers relating to *Orr vs University of Tasmania*, 1956, are in Tasmanian Supreme Court records, SLTA

85 · AKS 776

86 · Locher and Lake interviews

87 · Limerick ascribed to Bill Perkins, Scrivener interview

Chapter 6

88 · Wright, Narrative and Abstractions, AKS 761

89 · RD Wright, taped interview

90 · Narrative and Abstractions, AKS 761

91 · Wright to Orr, 12 March 1958, RDW 1/1/22

92 · Wootten interview; McAuley taped interview

93 · Wheelwright interview

94 · Berry memoir

95 · Orr to Wright, 12 December 1957, RDW 1/1/22

96 · Orr to Stout, 30 August 1957, AKS 488

97 · Orr to Stout, 28 January 1958, AKS 488

98 · Orr to Hodgman, 5 December 1957, RDW 1/1/9

99 · Graham to Stout, AKS 768

100 · 'Formal Finding and Observations of Scots Kirk Session on the Fama Clamosa Anent Professor Sydney Sparkes Orr', 27 June 1958

101 · Biggs to author, 23 September 1992

102 · Private evidence for the Scots Kirk, RDW 1/1/9

103 · Hills taped interview, UT 388

104 · Miller to Stout, 19 January 1958, AKS 485

105 · Wright to UK Association of University Teachers, 24 June 1958, AKS 751

106 · Wright to Eddy, 14 January 1959, RDW 1/1/13

107 · Hodgman interview

108 · Wright, 'A Reply to JR Kerr QC & JH Wootten', *Free Spirit*, September 1958

109 · Wright notes, RDW 1/1/6

110 · Rothfield interview

111 · Rothfield statement, RDW 1/1/7

112 · Gershon statement, RDW 1/1/7

113 · Orr to Wright, 26 January 1958, RDW 1/1/22

114 · Engisch statement, 18 March 1958, RDW 1/1/6

115 · Biggs to author, 23 September 1992

116 · Wright to Orr, 20 January 1958, RDW 1/1/22

117 · Montrose to Orr, 19 January 1958, RDW 1/1/7

118 · Wright to Montrose, 12 March 1958, RDW 1/1/22

119 · Montrose to Dunn, 6 May 1958, RDW 1/1/7

120 · Orr to Stout, nd February 1958, AKS 485

121 · RDW 1/1/6

122 · AKS 701

123 · Unpublished novel, The Cuckoo, RDW additional papers

124 · Orr statement, 9 January 1958, RDW 1/1/6

125 · Wright to Hodgman, 28 January 1958, RDW 1/1/6

126 · Anonymous letter, RDW 1/1/6

127 · Slessor to Wright, RDW 1/1/8

128 · Wright to Eddy, 2 January 1959, RDW 1/1/13

129 · Morrow to Stout, 23 March 1958, AKS 745

130 · Hutley to Stout, AKS 732

131 · Stout to University of Tasmania, AKS 485

132 · Armstrong to Gasking, AKS 485

133 · Stout to Day, May 1958, AKS 745

134 · Stout to Day, AKS 745

135 · Stout to Stout, October 1958, AKS 745

136 · Toulmin to Stout, 22 June 1958, AKS 745

137 · Ryle to Passmore, 13 November 1957, Passmore papers, ANL

138 · Stout to Rollins, May 1958, AKS 7

139 · Boyce Gibson to Stout, 28 May 1958, AKS 716

140 · Smart to Stout, 5 November 1958, AKS 732

141 · Partridge to Stout, 4 November 1958, AKS 732

Chapter 7

142 · J Kerr and H Wootten, 'A Rejoinder', *Free Spirit*, October 1958

143 · Wright to Champion, 9 February 1966, AKS 492

144 · Wootten interview

145 · Stout to Partridge, 12 August 1958, AKS 485

146 · Buckley to Scott, 17 July 1958, UTSA C8

147 · *The Dismissal of SS Orr by the University of Tasmania*

148 · Tanner to Diesendorf, 29 September 1976, Margaret Diesendorf papers, ADFA

149 · Tanner to Harwood, 19 May 1965, Gwen Harwood papers, UQFL

150 · Cranswick interview

151 · A Pavkovik (ed), *Contemporary Yugoslav Philosophy: The Analytic Approach*, Nijhof International Philosophy Series, 1988

152 · Wright to Buckley, 10 December 1958, RDW 1/1/11

153 · Wright to Eddy, 3 July 1959, RDW 1/1/13

154 · Orr to Wright, 30 December 1957, RDW 1/1/13

155 · Orr statement, 9 May 1959, RDW 1/1/22

156 · Eddy to Orr/Wright, RDW 1/1/13

157 · Horne interview

158 · Eddy to Orr/Wright, 27 December 1958, RDW 1/1/13

159 · Wright to Eddy, 5 January 1959, RDW 1/1/13

160 · Wright to Stout, 3 June 1959, AKS 485

161 · Eddy to Orr/Wright, 27 December 1958, RDW 1/1/13

162 · Wright travel diary, 29 October—5 November 1959, RDW 1/2/2

163 · Eddy to Orr/Wright, 5 October 1959, RDW 1/1/13

164 · Knopfelmacher to Krygier, 13 July 1958, Latham papers, ANL

165 · Eddy to Orr/Wright, 5 October 1959, RDW 1/1/13

166 · Eddy to Orr/Wright, 10 May 1959, RDW 1/1/13

167 · Eddy to Stout, 11 November 1960, AKS 733

168 · Wright to Eddy, 3 July 1959, RDW 1/1/13

169 · Eddy to Orr/Wright, nd 1959, RDW 1/1/13

170 · Wright to Eddy, 3 July 1959, RDW 1/1/13

171 · Eddy to Stout, nd, AKS 733

172 · Eddy to Stout, 1 November 1960, AKS 733

173 · Eddy to Clouston, 16 June 1959, RDW 1/1/13

174 · Higgins to Clouston, nd, RDW 1/1/13

175 · Macbeath to Stout, 5 September 1959, AKS 485

176 · Macbeath to Stout, 3 March 1960, AKS 740

177 · Wright to Montrose, 7 October 1959, RDW 1/1/7

178 · Gasking to Stout, May 1958, AKS 485

179 · Quoted in B Rish, The Tasmanian University Union, BA Hons thesis, 1981

180 · Harwood to Tanner, 10 November 1960, Gwen Harwood papers, UQFL

181 · Harwood to Tanner, 10 November 1960, Gwen Harwood papers, UQFL

182 · W Fletcher, transcript magistrates court, 28 January—5 February 1960, RDW 1/1/8

183 · Transcript magistrates court, RDW 1/1/8

184 · Quoted in *Advocate*, 5 March 1960

Chapter 8

185 · Eddy to Orr/Wright, 20 March 1959, RDW 1/1/15

186 · Clouston to Wright, 8 September 1960, RDW 1/1/13

187 · Wright to Clouston, 12 September 1960, RDW 1/1/13

188 · Clouston to Wright, 13 September 1960, RDW 1/1/13

189 · Orr to Wright, RDW 1/1/13

190 · Eddy to Stout, 23 December 1960, AKS 785

191 · Orr to Wright, 11 December 1960, RDW 1/1/13

192 · Eddy to Stour, 27 January 1961, AKS 733

193 · Eddy to Orr, 27 January 1961, RDW 1/1/13

194 · Eddy to Orr, 4 May 1961, RDW 1/1/13

195 · Eddy to Wright, 2 May 1961, RDW 1/1/13

196 · Wright to Eddy, 21 July 1961, RDW 1/1/13

197 · Comments on Brian Fitzpatrick's article, 18 April 1961, RDW 1/1/14

198 · Eddy to Orr, 18 November 1961, RDW 1/1/13

199 · Wright to Eddy, 21 July 1961, RDW 1/1/13

200 · Tanner memoir

201 · Macbeath to Stout, 3 October 1960, AKS 740

202 · Bishop to Wright, 15 November 1960, RDW 1/1/7

203 · Wright to Stout, 15 September 1960, AKS 734

204 · Wright to Stout, 12 December 1960, AKS 734

205 · Wright to Stout, 15 September 1960, AKS 734

206 · Wright to Orr, 14 November 1960, RDW 1/1/7

207 · Bishop to Wright, 15 November 1960, RDW 1/1/7

208 · Wright to Stout, 12 April 1961, AKS 734

209 · Registrar Queen's University to Isles, 25 September 1961, UT 175

210 · Montrose to Stout, 10 August 1960, AKS 485

211 · Ginnane interview

212 · Eddy to Orr, 18 November 1961, RDW 1/1/13

213 · Wright to Champion, 3 November 1965, RDW 1/1/20

214 · Ginnane, *Prospect*, 5, 1962

215 · Transcript of ABC interview with SS Orr, 1965, UT

216 · Miss G to Buckley, Mackay to Buckley and Buckley to Wright, RDW 1/1/22

217 · Buckley to author, 16 March 1992

Chapter 9

218 · Orr to Wright, 7 August 1964, RDW 1/1/22

219 · Orr to Wright, 25 August 1964, RDW 1/1/22

220 · Orr to Wright, 13 February 1965, AKS 487

221 · Stout to Rollins, nd 1958, AKS 745

222 · Fox to Stout, 5 September 1962, AKS 505

223 · Stout to Wright, 26 September 1962, AKS 510

224 · Wright to Stout, 6 February 1962, AKS 500

225 · Goddard to Stout, 24 September 1962, AKS 508

226 · Munroe to Stout, 28 September 1962, AKS 511

227 · Buckley to Wright, 18 September 1961, RDW 1/1/12

228 · McAuley taped interview

229 · Orr to Wright, November 1963, RDW 1/1/22

230 · Harwood to Tanner, 20 December 1963, Gwen Harwood papers, UQFL

231 · McAuley taped interview

232 · Taylor to Scott, 27 August 1963, UTSA C10

233 · Firth to Dallas, UT 516

234 · Stout to Orr, 24 December 1963, RDW 1/1/22

235 · Wright to Stout, 1 January 1964, AKS 555

236 · Jackson to Stout, July 1964, AKS 611

237 · Tanner to Stout, 4 May 1964, AKS 590

238 · Jenks to Thorpe, 13 November 1964, UTSA C10

239 · Orr to Wright, 8 December 1964, AKS 487

240 · Wright to Orr, 4 December 1964, AKS 487

241 · Orr to Wright, 17 September 1964, AKS 487

242 · Orr to Wright, 25 August 1964, AKS 487

243 · Minutes of the Scots Kirk session, December 1958, SLTA, NS 229/160

244 · Orr to Wright, 7 August 1964, AKS 487

245 · Orr to Wright, 22 June 1964, AKS 487

246 · Orr to Wright, 24 September 1964, AKS 625

247 · Orr to Thornton, 7 October 1964, AKS 631

248 · McAuley taped interview

249 · Orr to Wright, 4 November 1964, RDW 1/1/22

250 · Orr to Wright, 8 December 1964, RDW 1/1/21

251 · Smart to Stout, 10 February 1965, AKS 689

252 · Smart to Stout, 15 February 1965, AKS 690

253 · Rankin to Stout, 9 February 1965, AKS 686

254 · Hamblin to Stout, 17 February 1965, AKS 645

255 · Passmore to Stout, 17 February 1965, AKS 698

256 · Isles to Ashby, 27 May 1965, UT 339/196

257 · Wright to Orr, 21 May 1965, RDW 1/1/22

258 · Wright to Isles, 24 March 1964, UT 339/195

259 · Brett memo, 14 February 1966, UTSA C10

260 · Slessor to Wright, Wright and Hayes to Champion, RDW 1/1/22

261 · Wright to Orr, 31 October 1965, RDW 1/1/22

262 · Champion to Wright, 2 November 1965, RDW 1/1/20

263 · Transcript of special FCUSA meeting, 14 February 1966, UTSA C10

264 · Wright to Champion, 3 November 1965, RDW 1/1/20

265 · Firth to Smith, 7 November 1965, UTSA C10

266 · Wright to S Orr, 25 February 1966, RDW 1/1/22

267 · Wright memo, 14 December 1965, UTSA C10

268 · Medlin, 2 December 1965, UTSA C10

269 · Wright to Champion, 9 February 1966, RDW 1/1/20

270 · Transcript of special FCUSA meeting, UTSA C10

271 · Orr to Stout, 16 February 1966, AKS 488

272 · Wright to S Orr, 25 December 1965, RDW 1/1/22

273 · Notes on a letter, 18 November 1964, AKS 634

274 · Tanner memoir

275 · Carey memoir

Chapter 10

276 · R Davis, *Open to Talent*, Hobart, 1990

277 · Carey memoir

278 · Eggleston to Hytten, 11 January 1951, UT 47/126

279 · Hytten to Eggleston, 13 November 1951, F Eggleston papers, ANL 432/1/1142

280 · Eggleston to Hytten, 28 February 1952, F Eggleston papers, ANL 432/1/1156

281 · van Abbe to Morris, 16 October 1951, UT 47/126

282 · Hytten to Eggleston, 1 April 1952, ANL 423/1/1165

283 · Boyce Gibson to Hytten, 19 November 1951, UT 47/126

284 · Dallas memoir, UT 516

285 · Jennings interview

286 · Dallas memoir, UT 516, Firth interview, Kearney interview

287 · Dallas memoir, UT 516

288 · Stout to University of Tasmania, AKS 485

289 · Stout, 'The Orr Trials and Miss Kemp's Diary', *Observer*, 14 June 1958

290 · Thorpe and Buckley, press release 25 August 1958, UTSA C10

291 · Chappell to Polyani, 17 December 1956, UTSA C10

292 · Buckley interview

293 · McAuley taped interview

294 · Tanner memoir

COPYRIGHT

First published in 1993 by William Heinemann Australia

This edition published in 2021 by Ligature Pty Limited
34 Campbell St · Balmain NSW 2041 · Australia
www.ligatu.re · mail@ligatu.re

e-book ISBN: 9781922730695

ligature *un*tapped

This print edition published in collaboration with Brio Books, an imprint of Booktopia Group Ltd

Level 6, 1A Homebush Bay Drive · Rhodes NSW 2138 · Australia

Print ISBN: 9781761280825

briobooks.com.au

The paper in this book is FSC® certified.
FSC® promotes environmentally responsible, socially beneficial and economically viable management of the world's forests.